T0128575

ANTICHRISTS
AND THE
APOCALYPSE

JOSEPH POPE

WESTBOW
PRESS®
A DIVISION OF THOMAS NELSON
& ZONDERVAN

WestBow Press books may be ordered through booksellers or by contacting:

WestBow Press
A Division of Thomas Nelson & Zondervan
1663 Liberty Drive
Bloomington, IN 47403
www.westbowpress.com
1 (866) 928-1240

ISBN: 978-1-9736-8007-9 (sc)
ISBN: 978-1-9736-8008-6 (hc)
ISBN: 978-1-9736-8006-2 (e)

Library of Congress Control Number: 2019918826

Print information available on the last page.

WestBow Press rev. date: 11/22/2019

To the holy scriptures and many mentors who have moved me to "speak edification and exhortation and comfort to men" (Corinthians 14:3).

Contents

Preface

Most teachers will tell you that there is one in every class—a child who tests the limits and challenges authority. The student is not hyperactive or intellectually challenged. The terms *oppositional* and *defiant* come to mind—deliberate words and deeds of disdain for authority.

Lucifer, God's powerful angel, was such a creature; he was bigger, stronger, and smarter than the rest of the angels. His appearance was regal, magnificent. Like Lucifer, this super student quickly developed his own clique. He was smart enough to avoid being expelled from school. His God-given intelligence and superior memory ensured excellent grades. Most students would have been thankful for such natural talents and abilities but not Frankie. He was irritated by any authority that did not acknowledge his ideas and will.

Fast-forward thirty years. Frankie is now the Honorable Frank Meyer (a fictitious name). He is a successful politician having served with distinction in the military and as mayor of a European city. He now sets his sights on being prime minister of his country. During the debates, he easily runs circles around the other candidates. His masculine good looks and charming wife and children are admired by all. Only his wife knows the true nature of his personality and ambitions.

Halfway into his five-year term as prime minister, his wife is suddenly killed in a tragic airplane crash. Sympathy pours in from around the world. The investigation into the airplane crash is tightly controlled. Frank Meyer has learned to be proactive with potential P/R issues. He develops a trustworthy inner circle. Through demagoguery and deceit, the prime minister and his propaganda department weave a sanitized and polished portrait. The cult of personality develops and feeds his pathological narcissism. Some staffers are alarmed yet quickly learn to yield, if they wish to keep their jobs. He becomes increasingly inflexible. Any resistance is portrayed as unpatriotic or mentally defective. His need for approval and rigidity develops into a increasing circle of sycophants. Only the elderly recall the days of honest debate and objective evaluation. Truth is buried amid subjectivity and obfuscation.

Entrenched bureaucrats find ways to approve his policies. Discrete Gestapo tactics are used if all else fails. Again, history repeats, and Father God is not caught by surprise. Sophisticated bureaucrats feel superior as they cast aside the Bible as ancient literature and irrelevant to a modern scientific society. Soon, their conscience becomes seared as they repeatedly ignore sound doctrine. Soon, they are unable to discern truth and start embracing dubious human notions. Throughout history Scripture describes such people and advises the results of such thinking; "because, although they knew God, they did not glorify Him as God, nor were thankful, but became futile in their thoughts, and their foolish hearts were darkened. Professing to be wise, they became fools" (Romans 1:21–22). These people are actually usurpers and actually think they can commandeer God's creation. The great Tyrants of History are such individuals. However, this time, it develops as a worldwide deception. This time, technology enhances and reinforces deceptive autonomy. This time, Father God **_allows_** Satan to make his final move for worship.

CHAPTER 1
The Biblical Antichrist: Liar, Accuser, and Deceiver (LAD)

According to scripture, Satan was the original rebel. He was created along with "a supernatural order of heavenly beings, separately created by God before the creation of the world, and called spirits. Though without bodies, they have often been permitted to appear in the form of man…. Scripture describes them as personal beings, higher than humankind; …..they possess more than human knowledge, but are not omniscient ….they are stronger than men but are not omnipotent…..nor are they omnipresent….. at times, they are enabled to perform miracles…… Individual angels have different endowments and ranks (see Cherubim; Seraphim[1]and are highly organized".(1)

It seems Father God makes use of the church to teach angels and humankind that sin is toxic, and how to overcome sin (Ephesians 3:10). By existential knowledge, humans learn to recognize the wisdom of God. By vicarious observance of humankind via the church, spiritual entities learn the wisdom of God. Satan and his demons are our adversaries. However, humankind is enabled by the Holy Spirit and Scripture to overcome and live victorious lives. Victory, however, is determined by our choices during life.

If through Christ humankind can resist and overcome Satan,

---

[1] *Wycliffe Bible Dictionary*, 67.

so can spiritual entities. Sin always has consequences, though sometimes consequences are delayed. We are given time to reconsider and repent. As I recall from my college days, specifically my psychology of learning class, any delay between behavior and consequences decreases the effectiveness of learning. This is even mentioned in scripture: "Is it not because I have held my peace from of old that you do not fear Me?" (Isaiah 57:11). Others interpret delay as indifference, or worse, they mock God's existence. "The Lord God of their ancestors sent warnings to them by His messengers because He had compassion on His people and on His dwelling place. But they mocked the messengers of God, despised His words, and scoffed at His prophets until the wrath of the Lord arose against His people till there was no remedy (2 Chronicles 36:15–16; see also Psalm 78:35–42).

Some consider prophecy enthusiasts as members of the lunatic fringe. Will *you* be a scoffer or a mocker? The secular elites love to marginalize and dismiss devout believers. The trials and tribulations of this life cause some to become bitter. Others intuitively seek understanding and deliverance from our heavenly Father. I have found that faith in God always results in better outcomes. As I look back on my life, I can agree that "all things work together for good to those who love God, to those who are the called according to His purpose" (Romans 8:28). "The Lord is not slack concerning His promise, as some count slackness, but is long-suffering toward us, not willing that any should perish but that *all* should come to repentance" (2 Peter 3:9, emphasis mine). Remember, "But without faith it is impossible to please Him, for he who comes to God must believe that He is, and that He is a rewarder of those who **diligently seek Him**". Hebrews 11:6.

Satan's Antichrist is an attempt to present a counterfeit messiah. Will you fall for it? Satan's Antichrist is bogus, an imposter. Listen! This ability to discern deception is not easy. Especially if you are a 'carnal Christian'. (1 Cor 3:1—4, 2 Thess 2:11, Rom 1:28, 2 Tim 4:4) Because God and angels exist primarily in the spirit realm, the best way to relate to humankind is via a human body. That is why it was necessary for the Son of God to incarnate in our dimension of time and space. Satan will use deception and lies to present a false messiah. Years of apostasy have degraded this generation's ability to discern. Also, I believe the Rapture of the church will occur *before* the appearance of Antichrist.. Christians will not be here to sound the alarm. Hardened sinners full of pride and self-interest will be easy victims. But this world leader doesn't show his true colors until its to late. Like all Tyrants, he will become a control freak, and eventually demand worship (Daniel 11:31; Matthew 4:9; Revelation 13:8, 12–15). Even so, Scripture indicates that deceived humankind will *eagerly worship* the beast (Revelation 13:3–8).

In addition to LAD, (Liar, Accuser, Deceiver) scripture gives us many names and personality traits for Satan. These include; enemy, evil spirit, tempter, murderer, adversary, and unclean spirit. When I see a pattern of speech and behavior reflecting the above traits, I know that an evil spirit is behind the scenes. Godly discernment gives us the ability to accurately evaluate people and situations. We all need Godly wisdom and knowledge in our daily interactions.

Wycliffe Bible Dictionary gives further insight into this wicked being.

> He dominates all kingdoms of mankind, seeking their alienation from God and desires their destruction ... Satan's attempt to win over the allegiance of angels and mankind may thus have precipitated his loss of angelic status, for both the serpent and the humans were cursed simultaneously. But while man received hope of reconciliation to God, the Tempter was condemned to be trampled and crushed ... Satan incites people to evil, and is able to disguise himself as an angel of light ... the prince of the power of this terrestrial air; but, if we resist the devil he will flee from us

(James 4:7, conditions apply) … With the return of Christ, Satan is to be bound, that he "deceive the nations no more, till the thousand years should be fulfilled" (Revelation 20:2–3).

His final release will accomplish only the *destruction* of those he deceives, after which he is cast into the lake of fire forever. (Revelation 20:9–10; emphasis mine)[2]

Can you see why Satan is as mad as Hades?

According to John the apostle, we have entered the last hour of human history (since the beginning of the church age; 1 John 2:18–22). John provided behaviors and ideology that identified those with Antichrist traits. There will be a proliferation of Antichrists in the last days. Often, they pretend to be Christian, but they always abandon scripture for selfish reasons. "He is antichrist who denies the Father and the Son" (1 John 2:22).

I cannot stress enough that we must be on guard for deception (Matthew 24:4). Are the person's words and deeds in harmony with scripture? Do the words and deeds bring glory to God or self? What is the 'fruit' of the person or ministry? Matt 7:16 Do you sense peace or uneasiness? Finally, our 'due diligence' should include seeking godly counselors. (Proverbs 11:14, 24:6).

Brothers and sisters, immerse yourself in scripture.

It is the only way to discern truth from error. "Beloved, do not believe every spirit, but *test* the spirits, whether they are of God; because many false prophets have gone out into the world. By this you know the Spirit of God: Every spirit that confesses that Jesus Christ has come in the flesh is of God, and every spirit that does not confess that

---

[2] *Wycliffe Bible Dictionary*, 1529.

Jesus Christ has come in the flesh is *not* of God.
And this is the spirit of antichrist, which you have
heard was coming, and is *now* already in the world"
(1 John 4:1–3; emphasis mine)

John talked about how love was the defining characteristic of genuine believers: "By this all will know that you are my disciples, if you have *love* one for another (John 13:35; emphasis mine).

Dear reader, do you know the biblical definition of love? Try to define it before I quote scripture. Is it difficult to explain concepts such as love? Now compare your idea with scripture.

> "Though I speak with the tongues of men and of angels, but have not *love,* I have become as sounding brass or a clanging cymbal. And though I have the gift of prophesy, and understand all mysteries and all knowledge, and though I have all faith, so that I could remove mountains, but have not love, I am *nothing.* And though I bestow all my goods to feed the poor, and though I give my body to be burned, but have not love, it profits me *nothing.* Love suffers long and is kind; love does not envy; love does not parade itself, is not puffed up; does not behave rudely, does not seek its own, is not provoked, thinks no evil; does not rejoice in iniquity, but rejoices in the truth; bears all things, believes all things, hopes all things, endures all things. Love never fails." (1 Corinthians 13:1–8; emphasis mine)

The only love the Antichrist has is deceptive love. This ancient conflict between good and evil is referred to in Genesis: "And I will put enmity between you and the woman, And between your seed and her *seed;* He shall bruise your head, and you shall bruise His heel" (Genesis 3:15, emphasis mine).

Additional names and references to the Antichrist include the following.

- "little horn" on the fourth beast of Daniel 7:7–8
- "the prince that shall come" in Daniel 9:26
- "one who makes desolate" (like Hitler and other antichrists) in Daniel 9:27
- the "willful king" in Daniel 11:36–39
- "man of sin" and "son of perdition" in 2 Thessalonians 2:3
- the "lawless one" in 2 Thessalonians 2:8
- the "beast" in Revelation 13

Combining these names and descriptions of the Antichrist with liar, accuser, and deceiver gives you a detailed portrait of the coming Antichrist. The final Antichrist appears at the end of the church age. This counterfeit messiah is possessed and controlled by Satan. Corrupted and sinful humankind will swallow the deception easily due to decades of willful apostasy. Deliberate and persistent sin always develops into darkness or impaired reasoning (Romans 1:21, 22, 28; Ephesians 4:18; Isaiah 9:2; John 8:12; 1 John 2:11).

Is there a comparison between spiritual and physical sickness? Do physical illnesses mimic spiritual illnesses? For example, are the developmental stages of an addiction similar to the developmental stages of spiritual strongholds? Also, consider the general pattern of cancer cells. Healthy cells contribute to the health and welfare of the body. Cancer cells are autonomous and replicate only themselves creating tumors. Tumors are not concerned about the welfare of the body and serve only to 'search and destroy' healthy tissue. If not treated with strong measures (chemo-therapy, radiation therapy, surgery, ect), death is imminent. If sin is not dealt with via repentance and forgiveness, it will spread, and metastasize. It is very important to cultivate health habits such as bible study, prayer and fellowship with other believers. Another analogy is our 'immune system'. Spiritually, our immune system is strengthened by being 'doers of the word, and not hearers only" James 1:22—25. Our immune system will normally fight diseases such as cancer, but if the immune system is compromised, the cancer will spread more rapidly.

Our immune system is enhanced by faith and dependence on God almighty. As we yield ourselves to Christ, more and more of our spirit and soul are filled with the Holy Spirit. Spiritually, we cleanse ourselves by daily habits such as confession: "If we confess our sins, He is faithful and just to forgive us our sins and to cleanse us from ALL unrighteousness" (1 John 1:9). Failure to maintain our spiritual health—faith in God—can lead to opportunistic demons. In the same way, failure to maintain our physical health can lead to opportunistic diseases. To develop into a reprobate is akin to the stages of physical diseases. Those who allow sin to progress and develop risk their eternal souls as well as their physical health. Without spiritual focus and discipline, careless sinners could eventually become unfit and disapproved of. Theologically,

> "Reprobation is the condemnation of the lost to eternal separation from God ... In His efficacious grace, God is the credible cause of the salvation of the elect. He is not, however, the cause of the wicked being lost, for they are the chargeable cause of their own reprobation. They are "vessels of wrath who have fitted themselves for destruction." (Romans 9:22, literal trans.)

> Man is held responsible by God for his sin and for his rejection of God's way of salvation. God is not however obligated to overcome man's total depravity and save him by efficacious grace because that is an unmerited favor given by God only to those who He chooses." (*Wycliffe Bible Dictionary*, 1454).

Therefore, the only remedy for reprobates is removal from healthy believers.

The parable of the wheat and the tares (Matthew 13:24–30) indicates God allows the seed of the woman (Christians) and your seed (Satan's children) to coexist until the harvest. Another parable, Christ's judgment of the nations (Matthew 25:31–46), harmonizes with the parable of the wheat and the tares. The tares and the goat nations suffer severe punishment. The reasons for their punishment are given in each parable.

Father God gives us an entire lifetime to figure out the meaning of life and make our choices. Our words and deeds confirm which god, or God we honor. Because of our words and deeds, God's judgment will be fair and final. All our money, political connections, and talents will do nothing to sway God's righteous judgment. It is easy to take the path of least resistance: "Wide is the gate and broad is the way that leads to destruction, and there are many who go in by it" (Matthew 7:13). Don't fall for Satan's philosophy: "It's my life. I'll do as I want. Religion is fantasy dreamed up by demented old men. Only weak people need a God."

Dear reader, when you pass from this life to the spirit realm, it will be too late to make a decision. You had your chance. Hopefully you will not be shocked and saddened when you stand before the judgment seat of God. Hopefully you will not be like the condemned who survive the tribulation to see the second coming of Christ. Could this be the reason "all the tribes of the earth will MOURN, and they will see the Son of Man (Jesus) coming on the clouds of heaven with power and great glory"? (Matthew 24:30 "emphasis added"). Could it be that the mourners will be those who lived for self, those who decided to go for the gusto rather than a life of self-control and service to God?

Do you rebel at the thought of accountability to God? Human arrogance knows no bounds. Modern intellectual types consider accountability to a God as foolishness, fable, and, folklore. This generation, which is oblivious to the many signs and birth pangs, recoils at the thought of yielding to religious 'hocus-pocus'. They believe they have 'evolved' and are too sophisticated, educated, and self-sufficient to fall for 'primitive religious ideas'.

Father God knew this would happen.

> "Why do the nations rage, and the people plot a vain thing? The kings of the earth set themselves, And the rulers take counsel together, against the Lord and against His Anointed (Messiah), saying, Let us break Their bonds in pieces And cast away Their cords from us." He who sits in the heavens shall laugh; The Lord shall hold them in derision. Then He shall speak to them in His wrath, And distress them in His deep displeasure". (Psalm 2:1–5)

> Atheists claim God does not exist, but they spend a lifetime fighting theistic constructs. Could it be that deep down they believe? "Even the demons believe—and tremble!" (James 2:19). Yet they refuse to bend the knee to God.

All Seekers of God, Accept Christ as Your Lord and Savior

1. Admit you are a sinner.
2. Agree with God and turn (repent) from known sin.
3. By faith, believe that Jesus suffered and died to pay for your sins.
4. Prayerfully invite Jesus into your heart as your Lord and Savior.

Prayer

Dear God, I believe that your Son, Jesus, suffered and died on the cross to pay for my sins. Through faith in Christ, I accept Jesus as my Lord and Savior. Thank you for forgiving me and cleansing me from all sin. Help me to live for you and depend on you all the days of my life, amen.

This segment will detail selected kings and rulers in history who have taken counsel together against the Lord and against His anointed (Psalm 2:2). They were precursors and forerunners of the final Antichrist. They were cruel tyrants, sadistic, "without natural affection" (2 Timothy 3:3 KJV), "full of envy, murder … deceit … violent, proud … unloving, unforgiving, unmerciful" (Romans 1:29, 30, 31). They could not have cared less about human suffering. They considered themselves the elites and treated their people as less than farm animals.

There are many such people in history, for example, Joseph Stalin, Adolph Hitler, and Mao Zedong. More recent examples are Pol Pot, Kim Jong-il, Saddam Hussein, and Jim Jones. For those who do not know, Pol Pot, according to Wikipedia, was "a Cambodian communist revolutionary and politician who 'served' as the General Secretary of the Communist Party of Kampuchea from 1963 to 1981."

The Pol Pot Khmer Rouge government forcibly destroyed Cambodian society and forced most urban dwellers to march into collective farms. Many died of starvation or were executed and buried in mass graves, which became known as the Killing Fields. Their agrarian socialist utopia never materialized.

> Modern research has located 20,000 mass graves from the Khmer Rouge era all over Cambodia. Various studies have estimated the death toll at between 740,000 and 3,000,000—most commonly arriving at figures between 1.7 million and 2.2 million, with perhaps half of those deaths being due to executions, and the rest being attributable

to starvation and disease. (3). (https://en.wikipedia.
org/wiki/Pol_Pot)

The reader is referred to Wikipedia for more details, but the unspeakable atrocities and cruelty of Pol Pot and the Khmer Rouge is difficult to read.

Next is Jim Jones, an American religious leader. I was in my twenties when this man came on the scene; he killed himself in 1978. His name became synonymous with the Antichrist in my thinking. If Christians would only read and study the Bible, they would never be misled as his followers were. Unfortunately, Jim Jones was an excellent con artist and used and abused his people. The following quotes are taken from Wikipedia (https://en.wikipedia.org/wiki/Jim_Jones).

> James Warren Jones (May 13, 1931–November 18, 1978) was an American religious cult leader who initiated and was responsible for a mass suicide and mass murder in Jonestown, Guyana. Jones was ordained as a Disciples of Christ pastor, and he achieved notoriety as the founder and leader of the Peoples Temple cult ... In 1978, media reports surfaced that human rights abuses were taking place in the Peoples Temple in Jonestown. United States Congressman Leo Ryan led a delegation into the commune to investigate what was going on; Ryan and others were murdered by gunfire while boarding a return flight with defectors. Jones subsequently committed a mass murder—suicide of 918 of his followers, 304 of whom were children, almost all by cyanide poisoning via Flavor Aid ... According to religious studies professor Catherine Wessinger, while Jones always spoke of the social gospel's virtues, he chose to conceal that his gospel

was actually COMMUNISM until the late 1960's. By that time Jones began at least partially revealing the details of his "Apostolic SOCIALISM" concept in Temple sermons. He also taught that "those who remained with the opiate of religion had to be brought to enlightenment—SOCIALISM." Jones often mixed these ideas, such as preaching that, "If your born in capitalist America, racist America, fascist America, then your born in SIN. But if your born in SOCIALISM, your NOT born in sin." By the early 1970's, Jones began deriding traditional Christianity as "fly away religion," rejecting the Bible as being a tool to oppress women and non—whites, and denouncing a "Sky God" who was no God at all. Jones wrote a booklet titled "The Letter Killeth," criticizing the King James Bible. Jones also began preaching that HE was the reincarnation of Gandhi, Father Divine, Jesus, Gautama Buddha, and Vladimir Lenin ... In one sermon, Jones said, "Your gonna help yourself, or you'll get no help! There's only one hope of glory; that's within you! Nobody's gonna come out of the sky! There's no heaven up there! We'll have to make heaven down here!" ... Jonestown was promoted as a means to create both a "socialist paradise" and a "sanctuary" from the media scrutiny in San Francisco. Jones purported to establish Jonestown as a benevolent model communist community stating, "I believe we're the purest communists there are." In that regard, like the restrictive emigration policies of the Soviet Union, Cuba, North Korea and other communist states, Jones did NOT permit members to leave Jonestown ... While Jones banned sex among Temple members outside of marriage, he voraciously engaged in sexual relations with both male and female Temple members. (4)

Next, Kim Jong-il.

Kim Jong-il was the second Supreme Leader of North Korea. He ruled from the death of his father Kim Il-sung, the first Supreme Leader of North Korea, in 1994 until his own death in 2011. He was an unelected dictator and was often accused of human rights violations." All quotes taken from https://en.wikipedia.org/wiki/Kim_Jong-il . "the government began building a personality cult around him patterned after that of his father, the 'GREAT LEADER.' Kim Jong-il was regularly hailed by the MEDIA as the "FEARLESS LEADER" and "the great successor to the revolutionary cause." He emerged as the most powerful figure behind his father in North Korea ... Kim Jong-il was often the center of attention throughout ordinary life in the DPRK (Democratic People's Republic of Korea). On his 60th birthday (based on his official date of birth), mass celebrations occurred throughout the country on the occasion of his Hwangap. In 2010, the North Korean media reported that Kim's distinctive clothing had set worldwide fashion trends ... The song "No Motherland Without You," sung by the KPA State Merited Choir, was created especially for Kim in 1992 and is frequently broadcast on the radio and from loudspeakers on the streets of Pyongyang ... Kim Jong-il demanded absolute obedience and agreement from his ministers and party officials with no advice or compromise, and he viewed any slight deviation from his thinking as a sign of DISLOYALTY ... According to a 2004 Human Rights Watch report, the North Korean government under Kim was "among the world's MOST REPRESSIVE governments," having up to 200,000 political prisoners according to U.S. and South Korean officials, with no freedom of the press or religion, political opposition or equal education: "Virtually every aspect of political, social, and economic life is controlled by the government." Kim's government was accused of "crimes against humanity" for its alleged culpability in creating and prolonging the 1990' famine" ... By the 1980's, North Korea began to experience severe economic stagnation. Kim Il-sung's (father) policy of *Juche* (self-reliance) cut the country off from almost all external trade, even with its traditional partners ... Kim involved his country in state terrorism and strengthened the role of the military by his *Songun* ("military-first") politics ... Kim was known as a skilled and manipulative diplomat ... In 2000, after a meeting with Madeleine Albright, he agreed to a moratorium on missile construction. In 2002, Kim Jong-il's government admitted to having produced nuclear weapons since the 1994 agreement. Kim's regime argued the secret production was necessary for security purposes – citing the presence of United States nuclear weapons in South Korea and the new tensions with the United States under President George W. Bush. On 9 October 2006, North Korea's Korean Central News Agency announced that it had successfully conducted an underground nuclear test. (https://en.wikipedia.org/wiki/Kim_Jong-il) (5).

I could go on and on with the parade of sadistic tyrants from history. Can you see how the past is simply repeated? The future Antichrist will simply take advantage of a generation of malcontents and rebels. He will provide leadership for their pride, selfishness, and evil desires. This generation has long since loosed their moral anchors. Many have disdain for any authority except their own. This is nothing new, but biblical consequences always follow. Father God

> "gave them over to a debased mind, to do those things which are not fitting ... because they did not receive the love of the TRUTH, that they might be saved. And for this reason God will send them strong delusion, that they should believe the lie, that they all may be condemned who did not believe the TRUTH, but had pleasure in unrighteousness". (Romans 1:28; 2 Thessalonians 2:10–12)

Many of the current generation have gone beyond losing their way; they have lost any reverence for truth or God. Of course, for believers, Jesus is the "way, the TRUTH, and the life. No one comes to the Father except through ME" (John 14:6). God haters can't stand Christians who say Jesus is the _only_ way to God. How dare they claim that only one opinion is valid! But, Jesus said this, we only quote the bible. Brethren, "God is not a man that He should lie" (Numbers 23:19). Jesus never pleaded or tried to appease sinful man. In fact, to the contrary, Jesus said, "Do not give what is Holy to the DOGS; nor cast your pearls before SWINE, lest they trample them under their feet, and turn and tear you in pieces" (Matthew 7:6). Does the greasy-grace crowd find this offensive?

Any serious student of the Bible who sincerely seeks to know God, will find Him. I had to diligently seek Him for years. The prophet Jeremiah spoke of this; "And you will seek Me and find Me, when you search for Me with all your heart" Jer 29:13. Also; "I love those who love Me, and those who seek Me diligently will find Me" Prov 8:17. Like a diamond, His personality is multifaceted, regal and balanced. He can be robust, or gentle. He can be bold, or delicate. His personality is described in 1 Cor 13:1—13. He can be merciful, and He can exhibit tough love, when it is needed. He created the universe; what have you or I created?

We humans have a built-in 'defect' demonstrated by Adam and Eve in the Garden of Eden. Father God has provided a fix, a patch, or solution, but He will not force anyone to take it. The remedy is described in John 3:16 and Romans 10.

Let us move on. Question—is humankind born inherently good or evil? I want to state that historical evidence shouts that man is inherently evil. Have you seen toddlers whose favorite word is *"Mine"*! They will instinctively grab toys from younger siblings. Some toddlers have been known to bite, and inflict pain on those who resist their will. Social skills and Altruism has to be taught. Our souls—mind, will, emotions—have to be trained. Ultimately, we make our own choices. Like it or not, God will use our own words and deeds to judge us.

As readers of my first book—*Mr. President, I Respectfully Disagree*—know, I consider former President Barack Hussein Obama as a forerunner, or precursor of the final Antichrist. Of course, Obama did not rule with murder and mayhem. There are limits thank God in our open, mostly law-abiding society. He was elected twice by American voters. Yet I and many others were alarmed by his attempts to usurp or abuse the powers of the presidency. Most serious Christians were alarmed and outraged by his anti-Christian and anti-American words and deeds. In my opinion, Obama freely used nonviolent techniques and strategies to push his not-so-hidden agenda. He excelled at demagoguery. Definitions of demagoguery include;

> a leader who makes use of popular prejudices and
> false claims and promises in order to gain power.

SPECIOUS; having a false look of truth or genuineness. Superficially appears correct, but actually without merit. Possibly intended to deceive.

SOPHISTRY; Plausible, but subtly deceptive reasoning that is actually unsound.

OBFUSCATION; to make obscure, to confuse, blur, or muddy. To make more difficult to see or understand.

Several dictionaries offered these definitions including the *New World Dictionary of the American Language, Second College Edition* and www.merriam-webster.com.

Compare the above deceptive techniques to the biblical discernment techniques Jesus taught. The first chapter in my first book covered biblical techniques to discern good from evil. Matthew 7 is a good start. It is very important to place more emphasis on deeds rather than words. Deceivers and some politicians are experts at demagoguery—specious and spurious pontifications. Sad to say, but even Christians ministers are tempted to compromise and manipulate. There are bad apples in every field. Beware of those who use their oratorical talents to manipulate and dominate; some of them try to camouflage their true intentions. In my opinion Obama was good at this. Pray for the gift of discernment (1 Corinthians 12:8–10; Ephesians 4:7–11). You will need the gift of wisdom to use any spiritual gift. I highly recommend that my readers consult a good Bible dictionary in order to get a good foundation. Many years ago, I followed the directions of James and prayed for wisdom (James 1:5–8).

Numerous books and articles have documented the trail of Obama's lies, accusations, and deceptions. Allow me to list some of my sources; *Trickle Down Tyranny* by Michael Savage, *America's Most*

Biblically Hostile U.S. President by David Barton, *1,180 Documented Examples of Barack Obama's Lying, Law-Breaking, Corruption, Cronyism, Hypocrisy, Waste, Etc.* by Tim Brown (Freedom Outpost), *The Worst President In History* by Matt Margolis and Mark Noonan, and *Clean House* by Tom Fitton (Judicial Watch) among many others. Again, in my opinion, Obama had traits of the final Antichrist to come. Had it not been for our open, democratic, republican type of government, I have no doubt that the mainstream media, academia, liberals, progressives, activist judges, elite bureaucrats at the FBI, NSA, and DOJ, and entertainment elites, would have crowned Barack Obama ***KING!***

It has become clear to me that the bias and subjectivity of key leaders and bureaucrats can substantially corrupt any country. Satan uses corruption and mob rule to achieve his objectives. For activist judges, the law means only what each judge believes, not what the Constitution says. Unfortunately, the average middle class American simply swallows what the 'experts' say.

The Christian influence in America and the world has substantially dissipated. Similar to the decline and fall of the Roman Empire, we are following the stages of corruption, decline, and collapse. Dr David Jeremiah wrote about this in his book; *WHAT IN THE WORLD IS GOING ON?* (pages 134—138). Apostasy is similar to the rotting of an apple. The rotted part must be cut away. Unless a miracle happens—a revival—the United States is doomed. We have lost our way, and the vultures—the globalists, anarchists, socialists, and atheists —are eager to feed on our rotting corpse. Is this why America is not found in Bible prophesy? In addition to corruption and decline, there is another possibility for the demise of America. Could it be a ***sneak attack*** by the enemies of freedom? I will elaborate on this later in this book.

Spiritually we have progressed to a place of apathy, and pursuit of worldly pleasures. Formally taboo subjects are now often portrayed as normal and not to be judged. Males who 'think' they are female, are allowed into restrooms for little girls. We have gone beyond 'medical marijuana' to acceptance of recreational use of marijuana. Elections and the courts have condoned, or lessened penalties for use of drugs, porn, and 'unnatural' sex. Christian cleansing is passionately pursued, (prayer in schools, sports events, etc.), bible symbols in or on government buildings. The American family has become corroded with all kinds of sinful consequences including substance abuse, spouse abuse, child abuse, STDs, decreasing academics, runaways, and mental disorders of all types. But if the Israelites, God's chosen people, didn't repent and pray, what makes you think that Americans will get away with it.

Has God lifted His hedge of protection over America? Every day, America becomes more susceptible to economic forces, natural catastrophes, and new diseases. California, one of our most non-religious and progressive states, seems constantly in the news for one natural catastrophe after another. Who knows what else could happen? Could it be the debt bomb, Islamic terrorists with nuclear weapons, drought, fire, floods, earthquakes, hurricanes, Ebola, AIDS, antibiotic-resistant bacteria, viruses, or comet or asteroid impacts?

God is shouting via natural disasters, social disorder, and economic spasms that America is being chastised. It is a fact that Father God uses floods, droughts, pestilence, and other ways to punish wayward nations (Revelation 3:19; Jeremiah 3:3; 2 Chronicles 6:26–31; 1 Kings 8:35–40; Haggai 1:10, 11, 2:17).

For those who feel I am being unfair to Obama, let us look and examine his words and deeds during his terms in office. All of the following is documented from books and articles. Remember, Christ said, "You will know them by their fruits" (Matthew 7:16) and "By THIS all will know that you are my disciples, if you have LOVE for one another" (John 13:35). Remember the acronym **_L.A.D._** "Liar, Accuser, Deceiver".

1. In February 2009, President Obama trumpeted the Stimulus Plan and said it would "save or create 3.5 million jobs"

in the next two years (6). None of this turned out to be true. Did the news media hold him accountable? No. "We thought he was going to be the next MESSIAH" (7).

2. While running for President, Obama made a campaign promise to have all of the health care reform negotiations broadcast on C-SPAN. After being elected, that never happened (8). Sounded good and looked good, but it never happened.

3. On November 15, 2007, in Las Vegas, Obama said lobbyists "will NOT work in my White House." According to Tim Brown of Freedom Outpost, "By Feb 2010, he had more than 40 lobbyists working in his administration." (9) Yet his faithful never abandoned him. Another example of bait and switch.

4. Obama repeatedly claimed (lied?) that people would be able to keep their health insurance. Tim Brown of Freedom Outpost listed almost three pages of documentation to track this Obama 'promise'. This appears to be candy coating for the disastrous Obamacare health plan (10). At the time, most Americans were under the Obama spell. Those who should have held him accountable (news media, academia, government bureaucrats) carried his water, defended him, and never lost faith in him.

5. Obama repeatedly underestimated (lied?) about the cost of Obamacare. "In March 2012 the Congressional Budget Office said that over the next decade Obamacare would cost TWICE as much as what Obama had promised" (11). Typical empty rhetoric and deficit spending by irresponsible politicians who couldn't care less about the debt bomb. These increased entitlements may get politicians elected, but long-term consequences are inevitable.

6. In the category of deceiver (LAD), Obama administration officials had ***off the record*** meetings with lobbyists.

In June 2010, the *New York Times* reported that Obama Administration officials had held HUNDREDS of meetings with lobbyists at coffee houses near the White House, in order to AVOID the disclosure requirements for White House visitors, and that these meetings "reveal a disconnect between the Obama Administrations PUBLIC rhetoric—with Mr. Obama himself frequently thrashing big industries 'battalion' of lobbyists as enemies of reform— and the Administrations continuing, PRIVATE dealings with them." (12)

If true, the word *hypocrite* comes to mind.

7. In the category of accuser (LAD), the Obama administration accused two private businesses of being racist for using legitimate criminal background checks to screen employees (13). Who was the real racist here?

8. Continuing in the category of accuser, Obama criticized Mitt Romney for having investments in China and the Cayman Islands, but Obama has investments in both as well (14).

9. In categories of liar and deceiver, consider Obama's statements about same-sex marriage.

At California's Saddleback Forum in August 2008, when Pastor Rick Warren asked Obama's position on same sex marriage, the THEN candidate expressly said he was opposed to it because, as a Christian, he found it not in keeping with his biblical view of marriage. AFTER he was elected president, Barack Obama not only changed his view but went on to become the *cheerleader—in—chief* for all things gay (15). Classic bait and switch.

10. Again in the categories of liar and deceiver, consider Obama's statements regarding legislative pork or pet projects. In an edition of *Meet the Press*, Obama said to Tom Brokaw, "You know, the days of just pork coming out of

Congress as a strategy ... those days are over." Continuing to quote my source,

In February 2009, the Washington Post reported with something like wonder that the Stimulus Bill was not at all free of targeted pork "despite vows by President Obama that the legislation would be kept clear of pet projects."

Five years after the passage of the bill, Elizabeth Harrington of the Washington Free Beacon assembled a list of the ten "MOST OUTRAGEOUS" stimulus projects." This author will list only five; First; $152,000 for a study to prepare lesbians for adoptive parenthood. Second; $384,949 given to Yale University for a study entitled "Sexual Conflict, Social Behavior, and the evolution of Waterfowl Genitalia." Third; $1.2 MILLION for a study of erectile dysfunction in fat San Francisco–area men. Fourth; $100,000 to a Che Guevara (Marxist Revolutionary) inspired theater in Minnesota to produce "socially—conscious puppet shows." Fifth; $8,408 to Florida Atlantic University to test whether mice get drunk after consuming alcohol. (16)

More government tax and spend insanity. Does anybody read the bills they vote on?

11. Under the category of accuser, Obama accused surgeons of getting paid between $30,000 and $50,000 for a foot amputation, but Medicare pays between $740 and $1,140 for a leg amputation (17). Demagoguery? Inciting class warfare?

"Note those who cause divisions and offenses, contrary to the doctrine which you learned, and avoid them. For those who are such do not serve our Lord Jesus Christ, but their own belly, and by smooth words and flattering speech *DECEIVE* the hearts of the simple". (Romans 16:17–18)

12. Under the categories of abuse of office, enemies' lists, taking the fifth, supposedly lost emails, and shifting the blame, the Obama administration managed and oversaw IRS

employees who appeared to illegally target conservative organizations.

According to the Official White House visitor's log, during Obama's first four years as President, IRS Commissioner Douglas Shulman made 157 visits to the White House—This is more visits to the White House—by a very large margin—than ANY OTHER cabinet member during Obama's first term. By comparison, during the four years that Mark Everson was IRS Commissioner when Bush was President, Everson made only *ONE* visit to the White House. (18)

Almost nine pages of documentation were given by Mr. Tim Brown of Freedom Outpost, #170, 52–61/364.

13. Back to the categories of liar and deceiver:

In February 2013, Obama said "This is the most TRANSPARENT administration in history." At least two White House reporters and many others, including the Conservative, Non-partisan foundation *JUDICIAL WATCH,* disagree. "that same month (Feb. 2013) ABC News White House reporter Ann Compton, who covered Presidents Ford, Carter, Reagan, Clinton, both Bush's and Obama, said "The President's day to day policy development ... is almost totally opaque to the reporters trying to do a responsible job of covering it. There are no read outs from big meetings he has with people from the outside, and many of them aren't even on his schedule. This is different from every President I covered. This White house goes to *EXTREME* lengths to keep the press away." In July 2009 "White House reporter Helen Thomas criticized the Obama Administration for its lack of transparency." (19)

Judicial Watch has reported numerous legal battles with the Obama administration over the Freedom of Information Act requests. Is speculation really needed for why Obama did this?

I could go on and on. Remember his outrageous description of the Fort Hood incident as "workplace violence"? (20). Apparently, he was more concerned about offending Islam than American military victims. Recall the $50,000 payouts to people who often fraudulently claimed to be farmers (21), Obama's alleged mistruths about Benghazi, the stand-down order while people were under attack (22), and his recess appointments when Congress was ***not in recess*** (23). Imagine what Obama could have done in a totalitarian type of government.

Obama was a self-inflicted wound in that he was freely elected twice. The final Antichrist will also be a favorite of the people. Thank God, after the Obama administration, Americans have moved back to family values and common sense.

President Trump is not perfect, but he has the best interests of America in mind. He does not want to dismantle our Christian heritage. He does not want to tax and spend us into oblivion. He wants to protect border-state Americans who are suffering massive illegal entry into our country. He wants to turbocharge our economy, not regulate it to death. He seeks to terminate terrorists, not release them (Guantanamo). He seeks to support Israel, not marginalize a Jewish nation. He is a patriot, not a globalist. He seems to prefer the people controlling the government, rather than the government controlling the people.

Yet our federal bureaucracy appears corrupt and abuse of office appears widespread. Only God knows if America has enough strength to clean out the gangrene. This corruption is known by different names—the federal bureaucracy, the fourth branch of government, the deep state, the swamp, the shadow government, and the Obama/Clinton holdovers. Jay Sekulow, a renowned constitutional attorney and broadcaster, wrote about it in his book *Undemocratic—How Unelected, Unaccountable Bureaucrats Are Stealing Your Liberty and Freedom.* Jerome R. Corsi, PhD (Harvard University) wrote about it in his book *Killing the Deep State—The Fight to Save President Trump.* The divisiveness in America is more than a political battle; it is a ***spiritual*** battle. For some extreme progressives and Democrats, the concepts of reason and right and wrong are out the window. The prophesized apostasy is here. Moral absolutes are passé. Academia is guilty of brain washing our youth. (Satan is laughing). Some in the younger generation have no respect for anything Christian or patriotic. Have you noticed the increase in groups such as Antifa, and Fascist ideologies? Once again, history repeats itself. Will America simply be another blip on the dust pile of history? "If the foundations are destroyed, what can the righteous do?" (Psalm 11:3).

Brethren, I believe the great tribulation will strike like an ambush predator—suddenly.

> For it will come as a snare (trap) on all those who dwell on the face of the WHOLE EARTH ... Then they will deliver you up to tribulation and kill you, and you (Believer's) will be hated by ALL NATIONS for my name's sake. And then many will be offended, and will betray one another, and hate one another ... And because lawlessness will abound, (ANARCHY) the love of many will grow cold. But, he who endures to the end shall be saved. (Luke 21:35; Matthew 24:9–10, 12–13)

CHAPTER 2

Revelation 1–6: Revelation Examined

May I offer a possible scenario for the collapse of society and the rise of the prophesied world ruler. Again, I suspect that the nightmares of the tribulation will occur _**suddenly**_ as occurred with the _Titanic_ … Pearl Harbor … the Kennedy assassination … 9/11—_**suddenly!**_

Stage One

First, Father God raptures His family out of here. His paternal love for the faithful can be found throughout scripture. His pattern is to rescue and protect believers and their dependents. Often, His interventions are at the last moment. I believe the Rapture could occur just before a Nuclear War. Of course, this is conjecture. I doubt people will be making fun of 'doom and gloom' preachers at this time. Previous to the flood, Noah's generation thought he was a religious nutcase. Previous to the destruction of Sodom and Gomorrah Lot's generation was heavily invested in worldly pursuits and Lot was reluctant to believe the angels. Sound like today?

Imagine preparatory meetings between satanic globalists (Secret Societies?) in all parts of the world. Is the Illuminati real? Their devout messengers go out to selected government leaders. These secret elite members are servants of Satan. Nefarious plans are coordinated for maximum effect. Conventional, nuclear, and EMP devices are placed in strategic centers. Atheistic and pagan leaders maliciously plan with members of the secret elite. They eagerly anticipate assuming power beyond their wildest dreams. The plans unfold with success after success. The old established power structure implodes like an old building. Now, the Satanic conspiracy is in a position make its move.

After the initial shock, chaos develops as societal structures give way to disorder of every kind. In some places, communication is reduced to word of mouth. Widespread looting and anarchy break out. Due to the absence of electricity, stolen TVs, cell phones, computers, and appliances are worthless. After a few days, a mass exodus from jails, prisons, and mental institutions makes travel very dangerous. Only those with firearms and ammunition can travel, or protect their family. Dystopian movies come to mind, such as *Mad Max*.

Unrestrained violence, plunder, and even rape occur in plain sight. Raw panic and "men's hearts failing them from fear and the expectation of those things which are coming on the earth" (Luke 21:26). Paranoia replaces civility: "The love of many will grow cold" (Matthew 24:12). Gradually, the beast system of the Antichrist takes shape. The world is in chaos, and the 'Man of The Ages' makes his appearance. The entire world is suffering from PTSD, or, Post Traumatic Stress Disorder. A compassionate and fatherly person stands out. He proves his words with a restoration of law and order. He overhauls the world's economy. He subdues opportunistic warlords and tyrants. Gradually, the 'World Leader' earns the confidence and praise of the people. The masses do not realize the compassionate embrace is really the 'embrace' of a giant constrictor snake. Customary freedoms give way to 'Big Brother' surveillance and control policies. Every aspect of society is controlled. Anybody who disagrees with the 'World Leader' is re-educated, or, disappears. Again, Dystopian movies such as *Nineteen Eighty-Four* come to mind. What a horrible situation for those left behind! Why not seek God *now* before you are left behind?

Consider Accepting Christ as Your Lord and Savior

1. Admit you are a sinner.
2. Agree with God and turn (repent) from known sin.
3. By faith, believe that Jesus suffered and died to pay for your sins.
4. Prayerfully invite Jesus into your heart as your Lord and savior.

Prayer

Dear God, I believe that your Son, Jesus, suffered and died on the cross to pay for my sins. Through faith in Christ, I accept Jesus as my Lord and Savior. Thank you for forgiving me and cleansing me from all sin. Help me to live for you and depend on you all the days of my life, amen.

Revelation Examined

The following is prayerful speculation. It is beyond the scope of this book to attempt a verse-by-verse commentary on the Bible's book of Revelation. I believe Father God has always been willing to give insights to men and women throughout the ages. The Holy Spirit desires us to ponder and meditate on His Word. Many mornings during my Bible reading and devotional times, God gives me insights as I seek to understand His Word. He will do the same for you. Ask for understanding (wisdom) and He will give it to you (James 1:5). Only the Lord can enable us to "rightly divide the word of God" (2 Timothy 2:15).

Of course, no one can claim infallibility. If any of my words conflict with scripture, please disregard them. Our insights and ideas must pass certain tests. For example, are they in harmony with scripture and His revealed personality? Do they bring glory to God or self?

Sometimes, scripture interprets scripture. For example, "The seven stars are the angels of the seven churches, and the seven lampstands which you saw are the seven churches" (Revelation 1:20). After forty-plus years of Bible study, I know that context, common sense, and the still, small voice are very important; 1 Kings 19:12. Matthew 7, and Luke 11 teach us to "Ask ... Seek ... Knock." I have counted these three words in Matthew and Luke; *ask* is used eleven times, *seek* is used four times, and *knock* is used four times.

Earnest and persistent prayer is a fundamental principle of successful prayer. There are other principles of successful prayer as many of you know. Dr. David Jeremiah has taught on prayer. But let us return to Revelation 1:20. Seven is the number often associated with God. My sources report that seven represents perfection, and completeness (1). Angels are spiritual messengers that have different ranks and duties. According to scripture they are spiritual beings that can and do appear in our time and space dimension. Lampstands give out light so we can see. So, it is rather easy to understand the symbolic language of this passage. Are you starting to understand how to understand scripture?

I believe God has been, is, and will be constantly involved with the seven types of churches and seven church eras. In Revelation 2–3, He critiqued each type of church and church era. Revelation 4 starts off with

> "AFTER these things I looked and behold, a door standing open in heaven. And the first voice which I heard was like a TRUMPET speaking with me, saying, "come up here, and I will show you things which must take place AFTER this."

I believe that "After these things" and "after this" refer to the Church Age and the Rapture. If you do not know what these bible words mean, please consult a Bible Dictionary. Like a spent booster rocket, the church has accomplished God's assignment and falls away from the main spacecraft. The trumpet is a sound that cannot be ignored; it signifies that an important event, shift, or change is about to happen. Trumpets announce new milestones or eras that are about to occur. For example, other important God/humankind developmental stages include creation, the dispensations of innocence, conscience, human government, promise, law, grace, and kingdom.

The following is speculation as to how it may have felt for the apostle John as he experienced the intense spiritual vision known as the book of Revelation.

Suddenly you are in the Spirit. You are immersed in deep purple with glowing objects all around. You feel movement as you approach a massive structure. Mighty beings—angels—escort you to the throne room. Anticipation and consternation becomes overwhelming. Entrance to the throne room is by permission only. Your senses tell you that a powerful beam is scanning every thought, word, and deed of your life. Nothing can be hidden. You are warned to follow directions and not to speak unless spoken to.

You are ushered into a dazzling, surreal throne room including "four living creatures full of eyes in front and in back" (Revelation 4, 5, 6). Scripture describes it as follows.

> Immediately I was in the Spirit; and behold, a throne set in heaven, and ONE sat on the throne. And He who sat there was like a jasper and a sardius stone in appearance; and there was a rainbow around the throne, in appearance like an emerald. Around the throne were twenty-four thrones, and on the thrones I saw twenty-four elders sitting, clothed in white robes; and they had crowns of gold on their heads. And from the throne proceeded lightnings, thunderings, and voices. And there were seven lamps of fire burning before the throne, which are

the seven Spirits of God. Before the throne there was a sea of glass, like crystal. And in the midst of the throne, and around the throne, were four living creatures full of eyes in front and in back. The first living creature was like a lion, the second living creature like a calf, the third living creature had a face like a man, and the fourth living creature was like a flying eagle. And the four living creatures, each having six wings, were full of eyes around and within. And they do not rest day or night, saying: "Holy, holy, holy, Lord God Almighty, Who was and is and is to come!" (Revelation 4:2–8)

Wow! Steven Spielberg would be challenged to reproduce this scene.

I am told that communication in the spirit world is different. Thoughts and symbols are projected back and forth. There is understanding, but without words. God uses symbols to help earth dwellers understand Him. Symbols are like broadband instead of a telephone land line and carry much more information. Eyes to me speak of being conscious, alert, and intelligence. The eyes of these creatures scan and analyze in a way that is more powerful than any CAT scan or x-ray. These throne room creatures instantly analyze who you are, what you are, and every detail of your history, motivations, and intentions. No one gets into God's throne room without being examined.

And then it happens. You see Him. "And He who sat there was like a jasper and a sardius stone in appearance; and there was a rainbow around the throne, in appearance like an emerald" (Revelation 4:3). The colors are intense—deep orange-red, yellow, and brown along with a green rainbow. You immediately feel sinful, unworthy, weak. It is almost more than you can bear. Anxiety turns into panic. You feel your body losing control. You are reminded that you were invited, and an angel touches you giving you much needed reassurance and strength. You are told that you are allowed to see events soon to occur on earth. You look around and see thousands of angels and other spiritual creatures. Just when you are regaining strength, your senses are overwhelmed by **_lightning, thunder, and voices._** You are standing in front of seven lamps of fire, the seven Spirits of God. You feel like a worm among such powerful sights and sounds. You are totally vulnerable. But you are reassured again.

Okay, let's return to earth. What could these scriptures mean? The following are my thoughts. The sea of glass could signify stability. Earths Oceans and seas are tempestuous and dangerous. Glass can be transparent and stable. Strong glass can be walked upon safely. Transparency could speak of honesty and genuineness.

The number four is the number of the earth (2). There are four directions, four seasons, and four oceans. These four living creatures could be high-ranking heavenly agents assigned to mankind and earth. Their attributes speak of God's attributes and His dealings with earth and humankind. First is a lion, which speaks of strength, authority, and sovereignty. God is our King, and He wants us to advance into righteous strength and delegated authority. Second is a calf. Cattle speak of service and utility. God, the great provider, wants man to "subdue it (earth); have dominion over.....every living thing that moves on the earth" Gen 1:28. Third is the face of a man. God is a personal being capable of relational interaction. God is a multifaceted trinity. Humankind was created in the image of God with a spirit, soul, and body. Man is capable of fellowship with God. Fourth is a flying eagle. God is not bound by natural laws. He wants humankind to achieve and be transformed into higher spiritual creatures. Only those who overcome are granted access to spiritual evolution. The metamorphosis of a caterpillar into a Butterfly speaks of this. "Many are called, but few are chosen" (Matthew 22:14; Revelation 2:7, 11, 17, 26, 3:5, 12, 21).

"And there was a rainbow around the throne, in appearance like an emerald." Most scholars agree that the rainbow speaks of compassion and reassurance after the flood of Noah. The color green could speak of health and vitality. "Around the throne were 24 thrones, and on the thrones I saw 24 elders sitting, clothed in white robes; and they had crowns of gold on their heads." Again, according to my sources, the numbers twelve and twenty-four could represent divine government or priesthood (3). These twenty-four elders are overcomers, chosen as official agents of Father God. The number twenty-four is a multiple of twelve, and there were twelve tribes of Israel and twelve apostles. The temple had twelve gates and twelve foundations, and there are twelve months in the year. The number thirteen is often associated with sin and rebellion (4). Regarding the seven Spirits of God, two scriptures could help explain this.

> The Spirit of the Lord shall rest upon Him, The Spirit of wisdom and understanding, The Spirit of counsel and might, The Spirit of knowledge and of the fear of the Lord. (Isaiah 11:2, total of seven)

Jesus spoke of the Spirit of truth in John 14:16–17. This is no doubt the Holy Spirit and encompasses all seven Spirits of God.

Brethren, no one can claim 100 percent accuracy when commenting on scripture. I am trusting Father God to give anointed commentary. You should jettison anything unscriptural. In Revelation 5, we read, "Him who sat on the throne" (Father God), "A scroll" (seven seals prophesy), "So I wept much, because no one was found worthy to open and read the scroll, or to look at it."

As a longtime mental health worker, I realized that the apostle John was in a heightened emotional state. This often happens during times of extreme stress, crisis, and trauma. During my career as a screener, I completed thousands of mental health psychosocial and mental status interviews. I learned that when a client paused and became silent, or wept, or other emotions, I had touched a source of the stress and trauma.

Dear reader, imagine if **you** were in God's throne room! This scroll was so important that no one was allowed to look at it, let alone open it. That caused John to burst into tears.

> But one of the elders said to me, "Do not weep. Behold, the Lion of the tribe of Judah, the Root of David, has prevailed to open the scroll and to loose its seven seals." And I looked, and behold, in the midst of the throne and of the four living creatures, and in the midst of the elders, stood a Lamb as though it had been slain, having seven horns and seven eyes, which are the seven Spirits of God sent out into all the earth. (Revelation 5:5–6)

I hope you read the entire chapter. Notice that it says, "In the midst." Who but the second person of the Trinity could be in the midst of the throne room? Jesus is the Lion of the tribe of Judah and the Root of David. He is described here as the sacrificial Lamb. His suffering and death paid for our redemption and salvation. Only He was worthy and perfect as a sacrificial offering. Only Jesus met the criteria to pay for our sins. The number seven is associated with God. Horns are associated with power, strength, and dignity (5). The eyes in verse 6 are specifically designated as "the seven Spirits of God sent out into all the earth." Brethren, He observes everything and responds accordingly. I have said many times to my Sunday school members that sin is a big deal with God. Sad to say, but this generation seems blinded to the connection between sin and discipline. Many apathetic and complacent church members fail to see the urgency with 2 Chronicles 7:14 "If My people who are called by My name will humble themselves, and pray and seek My face, and turn from their wicked ways, **then** I will hear from heaven, and will forgive their sin and heal their land." I believe further judgments are coming, unless repentance and revival take place.

Unfortunately, most people are unaware of God's presence and

His dealings with us. Most have no idea that some circumstances (wars, natural catastrophes, extreme weather) could be a direct result of the law of sowing and reaping (Galatians 6:7). It is natural to be led by our sinful nature. They think no one is watching. The jails and prisons are full of such people. "The fool has said in his heart 'there is no God'" (Psalm 14:1).

Revelation 5:9 reads, "And they sang a new song." You will find a lot of singing in heaven. Music is a universal language with human beings; it facilitates communication, interaction, and relationship. It can lead to worship and mutual love between man and his Creator. Of course, forms of human expression including speech and art can be abused and perverted. Sex is a good example. Unrestrained anger is another. Thus the need for a 'user's manual' for humankind. Simple adherence to the Ten Commandments would solve much of our world's problems. God sent us His revealed will with guidelines via the Jewish leaders and prophets. There is only one tried and true, proven message from God—the Bible. Like it or not, almost all the writers of the Bible were Jewish. They were His chosen instruments. Listen! He makes the rules. Violate them at your peril.

I have a car poster or sign that can be fastened where vehicle state tags are displayed. In the middle of the printed message is a large picture of an open Bible and the words "When all else fails ... read the instructions." Yet thousands of Americans are defecting to the politically correct crowd and shedding their Judeo-Christian values like a snake sheds its skin. Father God is not taken by surprise nor is He amused! Revelation 5:10 identifies who will reign on earth. This occurs at the beginning of the thousand-year 'Kingdom Age'.

During the coming seven-year tribulation period, the forces of evil are forcibly removed by Father God. Believers, including kings and priests will be designated for service. The word *kings* probably refers to administrative and governmental duties. The word *priests* probably refers to religious duties.

I believe there will be regular humans (mortals) in the Kingdom

Age who will perform earthly tasks as they are done today. However, previous generations of human mortals who accepted Christ's offer of salvation will be awarded glorified bodies and will rule and reign with Jesus on earth (Philippians 3:21; 1 Thessalonians 4:13–18; 1 John 3:2; 2 Timothy 2:12; Revelation 5:10, 20:4–6). I have often wondered, whether, during the Kingdom Age, Christ will allow us to use modern technology. Or, if we will be required to live the old-fashioned way, similar to the Amish. I can't think of anything inherently evil about technology, but the terms and conditions of the Kingdom Age is up to King Jesus.

Let us look at the famous four horsemen of the Apocalypse (Rev 6). My secular dictionary (6) includes the following definition of apocalypse—"Any of various Jewish and Christian … writings depicting … the ultimate destruction of evil and triumph of good." My Bible dictionary (7) includes "an uncovering or unveiling … prophetic literature featuring end-time judgments of this world and visions of the next world."

The only worthy person, Jesus, the Lamb, opened the first seal judgment (chapter 6). One of the four living creatures said "with a voice like THUNDER, 'Come and see.'" John continues to be shaken to the bone with this powerful vision. "And I looked, and behold, a WHITE horse. And he who sat on it had a bow; and a crown was given to him, and he went out conquering and to conquer" (Revelation 6:2). Okay, who is this person, Christ? The first time I read this, I incorrectly identified the rider as Jesus. Men wearing crowns and riding white horses are usually the good guys. But not this time. I believe this person is a wolf in sheep's clothing, the Antichrist. Remember what Barbara Walters said about Barack Obama? "We thought he was … the next Messiah" (8). Let me first say that this character precedes the red horse of war, the black horse of economic collapse and severe famine, and the pale horse of death and Hades.

I believe Hades can be interpreted here as hellish effects that always result when humankind degenerates into total anarchy and unrestrained violence. It is clear to me, that man without God is an animal. The pale horse symbolizes the consequences of deception, war, famine, pestilence, and godless humanity.

The rider of the white horse, this **_seemingly_** good guy, did not obtain authority to rule in the usual way; rather, it was by intrigue: "A crown was given to him." Who gave him authority to rule? Could that be related to Daniel 11:21–45 ? Different Bible translations use the words *contemptible, despicable,* and *vile* to describe the Antichrist. However, this man is a master of deception. Remember that God looks upon the heart, not outward appearances (1 Samuel 16:7). No one can deceive God Almighty.

The final Antichrist, like Hitler, is careful to foster a cult of personality, a deceptive attempt to persuade the masses that he is a great man. But in his dark heart, he has a nefarious need to deceive and control others. His ego demands attention, service, and eventually, worship. The rider of the white horse has a bow but prefers to conquer by deceptive diplomacy, at first. He is a genius at persuasion. Remember the poem "Come into my parlor said the spider to the fly"? Mary Howitt (1799–1888) told

> the story of a cunning spider who ensnares a naïve fly through the use of seduction and flattery. The poem is a cautionary tale against those who use flattery and charm to disguise their TRUE evil intentions (https://en.wikipedia.org/wiki/The_ Spider_and_the_Fly__(poem).

"And in his place shall arise a vile person, to whom they will not give the honor of royalty; but he shall come in PEACEABLY, and seize the kingdom by INTRIGUE" (Daniel 11:21). Mr. 'Wonderful' will do what many others were not able to do. He will revive and reunite the old Roman Empire. I believe that recent history, specifically that of Hitler and World War II, could be one of God's final warnings. If we do not learn from history, we are certain to repeat it. Adolph Hitler intimidated and deceived most of Europe and notably former British prime minister Neville Chamberlain prior to World War II. Appeasement to a bully only incites contempt and aggression. Ronald Reagan, quoting Theodore Roosevelt said it best: "Speak softly, and carry a big stick." When my sons were little, and got on my last nerve, I would drape my belt around my neck. They knew I had given them their last warning, and they were much more cooperative.

Winston Churchill saw through Hitler's schemes and sounded the alarm. Churchill knew that Hitler's actions, not his words, spoke volumes. When Britain finally realized Hitler's true intentions, an unprepared and traumatized England immediately reversed course. Because of Germany's massive military buildup, it was essentially too late for a confrontation; many nations including France fell quickly. Due to isolationism, at first Roosevelt gave only token support to Britain. Even so, German U-boats sunk tons of equipment headed from America to Britain. America was reluctant to get involved in European affairs. However, the brutality of Hitler and Pearl Harbor, changed everything. How many times has God intervened at the very last second? It took several years, millions of young lives, and tons of military equipment to put down the maniacal Hitler. But the coming Antichrist will make Hitler look like a choirboy.

Most scholars agree that the red horse symbolizes war. I believe end-time wars will involve multiple ethnic wars on multiple continents. The current status quo collapses and a free-for-all breaks out to reconstruct the pecking order. Eventually, a New World Order emerges. Guess who comes out of the fray on top? Yep, the Antichrist's revived Roman Empire, as described in Revelation. Political dominance includes economic, religious, and military dominance. Because of deliberate worldwide apostasy, Father God allows evil to prosper … at least temporarily.

> The coming of the lawless one is according to the working of Satan, with all power, signs, and lying wonders, with all unrighteous deception among those who perish, because they did not receive the love of the truth, that they might be saved. And for this reason, GOD WILL SEND THEM STRONG DELUSION, that they should believe the lie, that they all may be condemned who did not believe the truth but had pleasure in unrighteousness. (2 Thessalonians 2:9–12)

We stiff-arm God at our own peril. People who delight in evil and refuse to repent will be judged accordingly (Romans 1:24–26; Mark 4:11–12; Jude 14, 15; Acts 12:23). We are even told, "Do not give what is holy to the dogs; nor cast your pearls before swine, lest they trample them under their feet, and turn and tear you in pieces" (Matthew 7:6).

War comes with consequences—economic distress, lower food production, problems with transportation, disease, pestilence, and social disorder. All resources are diverted to support the war effort and protect society. I believe it was Ronald Reagan who said that if we were defeated in war, all other priorities were irrelevant; thus the importance of a strong military. Social programs, welfare, Medicare, Social Security, and education have their place, but a strong military should be the number-one priority.

Let us continue to discuss these four horsemen.

> When He opened the third seal, I heard the third living creature say, "Come and see." And I looked, and behold, a BLACK horse, and he who sat on it had a pair of scales in his hand. And I heard a voice in the midst of the four living creatures saying, "A quart of wheat for a denarius, and three quarts of

barley for a denarius; and do not harm the oil and the wine." (Revelation 6:5–6)

What if the rider on all four horses is none other than the final Antichrist himself? His words and deeds result in misery, death, and disorder. He loves destroying God's creation. The Four Horsemen symbolize cascading plagues. Father God has lifted his protection due to persistent sin and refusal to repent. Instead of seeking God, the masses are taken in by the great imposter. He can't touch Father God, but he can deceive, maul, and brutalize His creation. But the story is not over. It's always the darkest just before dawn.

According the *Wycliffe Bible Commentary*, the *Ryrie Study Bible*, and others, a denarius was a Roman silver coin equivalent to a day's wage. This means that essentially it took a day's earnings to buy a loaf of bread. The results of war almost always include runaway inflation, famine, and disease; thus the black horse represents economic collapse and famine. Brethren, the Bible describes what ancient people did during extreme famine. I winced when I read it.

All Seekers of God, Accept Christ as Your Lord and Savior

1. Admit you are a sinner.
2. Agree with God and turn (repent) from any known sin.
3. By faith, believe that Jesus suffered and died to pay for your sins.
4. Prayerfully invite Jesus into your heart as your Lord and Savior.

Prayer

Dear God, I believe that your Son, Jesus, suffered and died on the cross to pay for my sins. Through faith in Christ, I accept Jesus as my Lord and Savior. Thank you for forgiving me and cleansing me from all sin. Help me to live for you and depend on you all the days of my life, amen.

If you have lived for any significant length of time, you know what "pale, gaunt, and sickly" means. When I see an old friend I have not seen in many months or years and he or she appears pale, gaunt, and sickly, the 'C' word immediately comes to mind—*cancer.*
The next horse is pale.

> "When He opened the fourth seal, I heard the voice of the fourth living creature saying, "Come and see." And I looked and behold a PALE horse. And the name of him who sat on it was DEATH, and HADES followed with him. And power was given to them over a fourth of the earth, to kill with SWORD, with HUNGER, with DEATH, and by the BEASTS of the earth."(Revelation 6:7–8)

I think many secular scientists recoil at the thought of a God. Scripture states; "Knowledge puffs up, but love edifies"………."Pride goes before destruction, And a haughty spirit before a fall." 1 Cor 8:1, Prov 16:18. Original sin infects all of us at birth with pride and selfishness.

The cure, or antidote, is humble submission, and acceptance of the true God. This should lead to a desire to know Him, and please Him. But many, including myself at first, would not submit to, or obey, an invisible entity. Thus they fail the 'faith test'. They are too proud to trust in God. If not corrected this could result in denial of His favor and blessings. Possible condemnation awaits those who refuse to believe "in the name of the only begotten Son of God" (John 3:18). They show by their choices that they will never acquiesce or respect Him. Yet, He allows a lifetime for this important decision to be made. Dear brethren, when you reach my age—sixty-nine—you will realize the brevity of life. Seek Him while there is still time.

I think the 'beasts' of the earth in Revelation 6:8 may have a twofold meaning. First, beasts often symbolize tyrannical governments that terrorize their subjects (10). Second, a beast can also mean someone who violently attacks believers. Violent persecution usually indicates satanic activity. Satan was behind the persecution of the Old Testament prophets, New Testament apostles, and of course Jesus.

All true Christians who do damage the devil's kingdom will quickly find out that Satan is real. In my opinion, all new Christians should go through an 'orientation class' to learn about Satan's activities. Brethren, we are in a spiritual war, and training in spiritual warfare is essential. In 1 Corinthians 15:32, we read, "If, in the manner of men, I have fought with beasts at Ephesus" (see also Jude verse 10; 2 Peter 2:12). So 'beasts' can also refer to ungodly men.

Christians and Jews are coming under increasing abuse and harassment and even outright slaughter. Scripture and history assure us that Father God will not tolerate this for very long. Persecution is one of a multitudes of signs, and birth pangs, that indicate Jesus will return very soon (Matthew 24:9). I recommend two of many good books on this topic: *40 Irrefutable Signs of the Last Generation* by Noah W. Hutchings and *The Book of Signs—31 Undeniable Prophecies of the Apocalypse* by Dr. David Jeremiah.

Speaking of martyrs, Revelation 6:9–11 describes these martyrs as under the altar shouting loudly for vengeance on those who violently killed them and separated them from their loved ones. Here, they are in the presence of Father God, and nothing has been done to those wicked people.

Verse 11 shows a kind and understanding God. In a fatherly manner, these murdered martyrs are given white robes and counseled: "And it was said to them that they should rest a little while longer, until both the number of their fellow servants and their brethren, who would be killed as they were, was completed." This exchange reinforces the reality of John's vision. Even in God's throne room, people blurt out their feelings. They apparently do not realize that God allows free will. Father God will intervene at the right time. Also, they forget that God's spiritual laws of sowing and reaping are always in effect. Judgment may be delayed, but it is never ignored. "Do not be deceived, God is not mocked; for whatever a man (or woman) sows, that he will also reap" (Galatians 6:7). Another factor is that fulfilled prophesy greatly reinforces scripture as the divinely inspired Word of God.

Revelation 6:12–14 leaves no doubt that the judgments and wrath of almighty God have finally been unleashed.

> I looked when He opened the sixth seal, and behold, there was a GREAT earthquake; and the sun became black as sackcloth of hair, and the moon became like blood. And the stars of heaven fell to the earth, as a fig drops it late figs when it is shaken by a mighty wind.

To me, this symbolizes both earth and heaven shaken by divine judgment; this is part of the finale. The Church Age is giving way to the kingdom age. The sun became black. Lights out!.......... Stars fell to the earth (Revelation 6:13). Could this be symbolism indicating that Satan and his angels are cast to the earth?...... "A fig drops its late figs when it is shaken by a mighty wind" (Revelation 6:13). Could this be symbolism indicating Israel (Figs) is shaken by God (Mighty Wind), for trusting in the Antichrist for safety?

Fast-forward to Revelation 12:7–9.

> And war broke out in heaven; Michael and his angels fought against the dragon; and the dragon and his angels fought, but they did not prevail, nor was a place found for them in heaven any longer.

So the great dragon was cast out, that serpent of old, called the Devil, and Satan, who deceives the whole world; he was cast to the EARTH, and his angels were cast out with him.

Again, Figs and the fig tree are symbols of the nation of Israel. As stated previously, stars can be symbols for angels or earthly rulers both good and bad. "A rushing mighty wind" represents the Holy Spirit in Acts 2:2. Here, we see Father God shaking both heaven and earth, both evil spiritual entities and evil earthly entities. God is overthrowing the old order and setting up a new order, the Kingdom Age. Did you notice the four names given for Satan? God **ALLOWS** Satan, formerly Lucifer, to wreak havoc on earth temporarily. No doubt heaven is glad to be rid of him.

My head is spinning. I am trying to put it all together. Sometimes, I get too close to the trees to see the forest. The thought came to me that each series of divine judgments—seven seals, seven trumpets, seven thunders, seven bows—speaks of God's righteous anger from four perspectives, just as the four gospels gave four different perspectives on the life and ministry of Christ.

Revelation 6:14–17 reads,

"Then the sky receded as a scroll when it is rolled up, and EVERY mountain and island was moved out of its place (Isa 13:6–10, 13) And the kings of the earth, the great men, the rich men, the commanders, the mighty men, every slave and every free man, hid themselves in the caves and in the rocks of the mountains, and said to the mountains and rocks, "Fall on us and hide us from the face of HIM who sits on the throne and from the wrath of the Lamb! "For the great day of His wrath has come, and who is able to stand?"

Deep down, humankind knows that almighty God is orchestrating these legitimate, righteous, and powerful judgments. Major life events are practical in that they force humankind to evaluate life. Trials and tribulations can cause us to become '**bitter, or better'**. It is much better to learn of God's favor and blessings as we experience life's up's and down's. One of my favorite scriptures states ; "Many are the afflictions of the righteous, But the Lord delivers him out of them all." Ps 34:19. Those who know the God of the Bible know that judgment follows apostasy like thunder follows lightning. The collapse of evil causes the righteous to rejoice. King David wrote of this in Psalms 3:7, 7:11–13, 18:34–42, and 21:8–13.

Celestial and astronomical terms are indicated in Revelation 6:12–17. How else can these earthshaking, global catastrophes be understood? It is always fascinating to explore God's creation in light of scientific disciplines. I love 'Nature' shows such as those on "Nova" and "National Geographic". I am not an expert in astronomy, meteorology, geology, asteroids, comets, or meteorites, but I can read and quote people who are. I know a little bit about the Bible and the God of the Bible. Only a fool could look at the complexity and precision of nature and say there was no God.

Brethren, use the brain that God gave you. Time and random chance are foolishness as credible creation models. Intelligent design is in evidence everywhere. Human pride is the problem; it is the signature evidence of Satan. Human pride stems from the god of this world, Satan (2 Corinthians 4:3–4). Thank God He is slow to anger (Psalm 145:8). He always gives ample time for men and women to make their choices, but repeated and prolonged patience can lead Him to proactive actions (Genesis 6:3).

God knows how to make life rough and bumpy for the unrepentant. Consider the plagues of Egypt, the flood of Noah's day, Sodom and Gomorrah, and the crushing judgments of the book of Revelation. Could it be that Revelation 6:14–17 and other passages are describing a mass extinction event? Matthew 24:22 reads, "And unless those days were shortened, no flesh would be saved; but for the elect's sake those days will be shortened" At least three versions of the Bible (NIV, NLT, HCSB) translate "saved" as "survive." I believe those designated for martyrdom and other believers will be present during the seven-year tribulation period. Because of the presence of His children, Father God will shorten those terrible days. This is consistent with His compassionate heart.

If you have not repented and yielded your life to Christ, please, do not put it off any longer. However, if the rapture has already occurred as you read this, you will need all the faith you can muster. But, as He did with Corrie ten Boom, He will go with you through it all. He will never leave you or forsake you. Death is simply a transition.

CHAPTER 3
Revelation 7–9

In Revelation 7, after earth dwellers realize that the end-time wrath of God has started, "I saw four angels standing at the four corners of the earth, holding the four winds of the earth, that the wind should not blow on the earth, or the sea, or any tree." Those alive at this time are probably moaning, "Dear God, what is this?"

Wind-driven weather has been part of the human experience since Adam and Eve. Imagine the stagnation and discomfort resulting from no wind. Before long, smog, smoke, and dust from factories all over the world would become noxious and suffocating. No more Mr. Nice Guy. The Creator is mad, and He is, once again, sending His plagues to a rebellious and sinful generation.

Only He could design such worldwide judgments. Only He knows the chronology of end-time judgments. Perhaps chapter 7 is simply another perspective on earlier judgments? But before this judgment is allowed to proceed, an

> "angel ascending from the east, having the SEAL of the living God ... cried with a loud voice to the four angels ... saying, "Do not harm the earth, the sea, or the trees till we have sealed the servants of our God on their foreheads." (Revelation 7:2–3)

This angel has God's official seal that designates the authority of God. This angel seems to abruptly enter the scene to ensure that God's servants are not hindered. Specifically, they are 144,000 messianic Jews who preach God's salvation message. The church age is over! The church has been raptured to heaven. Messianic Jews now make up for thousands of years of Jewish rejection of gentiles, and Messiah Jesus. The Jews are the natural branches. The root or vine is symbolic of God. The root or vine supports and provides life to the branches. Gentiles have been grafted onto the root or vine, in place of the Jewish branches. (John 15:4—7, Romans 11:17–26). I have observed many times that a Jew who recognizes Jesus as the Messiah is highly effective as an evangelist.

Next, we see the results of their efforts: "A great multitude … clothed with white robes, with palm branches in their hands" identified as "the ones who come out of the great tribulation, and washed their robes and made them white in the blood of the Lamb" (Revelation 7:9–15). White robes symbolize imputed righteousness. Palm branches symbolize worship. Washing their robes could symbolize martyrdom, or salvation. Finally, the blood of the Lamb symbolizes redemption.

Revelation 7:16 gives a glimpse of the severe suffering going on at this time—extreme hunger, famine, scarcity of drinkable water, and being fried by a disturbance in the sun. The talking heads of the mainstream media and academia do not have a clue concerning what is really going on. They parade 'experts' who try to explain the extreme weather, and solar disturbances. Also, they are busy praising the beloved leader who is active in social and humanistic efforts to ameliorate and relieve suffering.

In Revelation 8, we read, "When He opened the seventh seal, there was silence in heaven for about half an hour." Here, Father God is giving everyone, human and angelic, time to digest what has happened and a pause before what is about to take place.

Next, we see the importance of prayer. God hears the prayers of the saints; He can protect the innocent and punish the guilty during these terrible days of judgment. "Then the angel took the censer, filled it with fire from the altar, and threw it to the earth. And there were NOISES, THUNDERINGS, LIGHTENINGS, and a EARTHQUAKE" (Revelation 8:5). The effects of God's presence are given in selected passages of scripture. Compare John's perception of God (Revelation 8:5) with King David's description (2 Samuel 22:7–16). Remember, "our God is a consuming fire" (Hebrews 12:29).

> The first angel sounded: (trumpets) And hail and fire followed, mingled with blood, and they were thrown to the earth; and a third of the trees were burned up, and all green grass was burned up. (Revelation 8:7)

Hail to me symbolizes extreme weather. Plagues are either authorized by God, or allowed by God. Fire is the opposite of frozen hail. Biblical history reveals that drought and flood can be used as tools of God's judgment. The phrase "mingled with blood" speaks of violent deaths. Something, possibly nuclear warfare or a solar disturbance, causes extreme global weather disturbances. But the main effects here are hail and scorching heat that burned up a third of the trees and all the green grass. Trees are much larger than grass and can take more abuse. Something disturbs our sun greatly. Remember, God controls the sun, and He can and will make use of it to punish rebels.

Another possibility for extreme global weather disturbance is nuclear warfare. The following quote is taken from www.science20. com (*Climate Effects of Nuclear Weapons* by Ed Chen, November 3, 2010).

> "The effect of a Regional Nuclear War of only fifty 10-kiloton bombs upon the environment and the subsequent suffering produced by an abrupt change in the climate system, would be far more

devastating than problems caused by greenhouse gasses and ozone depleting chemicals, including massive famine and migration, poisoning of water supplies, severe drops in temperature of up to 20 degrees below average, and the destruction of the biosphere and the stabilizing effects plants have on the climate ... a nuclear conflict would create changes far worse than the general circulation models predict by quickly forcing the climate system into a new "regime" with terrifying consequences for agriculture."

"The second angel sounded: and something like a great mountain burning with fire was thrown into the sea, and a third of the sea became blood; and a third of the living creatures in the sea died, and a third of the ships were destroyed." (Revelation 8:8–9)

Does sea mean the Mediterranean, or all the oceans? Bible prophesy focuses mainly on Israel and the revived Roman Empire. I have always felt that these verses describe an impact event, a collision between an astronomical object and the earth. According to Wikipedia (https://en.wikipedia.org/wiki/Impact_event),

Major impact events have significantly shaped earth's history, and have been implicated in the formation of the Earth—Moon system, the evolutionary history of life, the origin of water on Earth and several mass extinctions. Notable impact events include the Chicxulub impact, 66 million years ago, believed to be the cause of the Cretaceous—Paleogene (Dinosaurs) extinction event. Throughout recorded history, hundreds of

Earth impacts (and exploding bolides) have been reported, with some occurrences causing deaths, injuries, property damage, or other significant localized consequences. One of the best known recorded impacts in modern times was the Tunguska event, which occurred in Siberia, Russia, in 1908. The 2013 Chelyabinsk meteor event is the only known such incident in modern times to result in a large number of injuries, excluding the 1490 Ch'ing-yang event in China. The Chelyabinsk meteor is the largest recorded object to have encountered the Earth since the Tunguska event. The asteroid impact that caused Mistastin crater generated temperatures exceeding 2,370 C, the highest temperatures known to have occurred on Earth. The Comet Shoemaker—Levy 9 impact provided the first direct observation of an extraterrestrial collision of Solar System objects, when the comet broke apart and collided with Jupiter in July 1994.

More specifically regarding the comet Shoemaker-Levy 9, another Wikipedia article stated,

> When fragment A of the nucleus entered Jupiter's southern hemisphere at a speed of about 60 km/s (35 mi/s) instruments on Galileo (American spacecraft) detected a fireball that reached a peak temperature of about 24,000 k (23,700 C; 42,700 F) … Over the next six days, 21 distinct impacts were observed, with the largest coming on July 18 at 07:33 UTC when fragment G struck Jupiter. This impact created a giant dark spot over 12,000 km (7,500 mi) across, and was estimated to have released an

energy equivalent to 6,000,000 megatons of TNT
(600 times the world's nuclear arsenal). (1)

Can you imagine being on earth during a similar impact event?

I believe Father God deliberately wanted mankind to see the incredible forces unleashed when the comet hit Jupiter. Twenty one impacts were observed. Twenty one is a multiple of **seven.** Seven is the number associated with God. Twenty one divided by seven = 3. Three is the number of the Trinity. The spacecraft Galileo *just happened* to be in route to Jupiter when this event occurred. Most of us today take our daily safety for granted. However, earth dwellers are very vulnerable. Non-believers do not realize that He controls our next breath. He holds the planets and stars in place. It was God who fine-tuned earth for the human habitation. In scientific circles, it is known as the Goldilocks principle. For a detailed look at this, see chapter 7 of *God of the Big Bang* by rocket scientist and Hubble Space Telescope engineer Dr. Leslie Wickman.

Hold on! There are more earthshaking events to come. Revelation 8:10–11 states,

> Then the third angel sounded; and a great star fell from heaven, burning like a torch, and it fell on a third of the rivers and on the springs of water; (fresh water) and the name of the star is wormwood; and a third of the waters became wormwood; and many men died from the water, because it was made bitter.

At first, I thought this was another impact event. But upon further examination, I believe it could be an angel similar to the death angel of 1 Chronicles 21:15, 2 Samuel 24:16, and Exodus 12:23. How else could an impact event focus specifically on only a third of the rivers and springs? Dear reader, guess who has protected and provided safe drinking water for past generations? The difference is that Father God has removed His loved ones via the Rapture, and He now allows hardened sinners to experience life without His protection.

I want to remind the reader that the current lack of spiritual life and spiritual discernment is a major sign of the second coming of Christ (Luke 17:26–30, 37; 2 Thessalonians 2:3). Also, this generation has traits of some of the "seven churches which are in Asia" (Western Turkey) Rev 1:4. 1. "you have left your first love" (Ephesus) Rev 2:4. In other words, the zeal is gone. 2. "you have there (Pergamos) those who hold the doctrine of Balaam, who taught Balak to put a stumbling block before the children of Israel, to eat things sacrificed to idols, and to commit sexual immorality. Thus you also have those who hold the doctrine of the Nicolaitans, which thing I hate." Rev 2:14,15. In other words, liberal ideology with entitlement notions permitting religious and fleshly indulgence. 3. "I know your works, that you have a name (Sardis) that you are alive, but you are dead" Rev 3:1 In other words, a dead church, going through the motions, but, with 'dead works'. 4. I found the church in Philadelphia especially relevant to our generation. *"for you have a little strength, have kept My word, and have not denied My name. "Indeed I will make those of the synagogue of Satan, who say they are Jews and are not, but lie—indeed I will make them come and worship before your feet, and to know that I have loved you. Because you have kept My command to persevere, I also will keep you from the hour of trial which shall come upon the whole world, to test those who dwell on the earth. "Behold, I come quickly! Hold fast what you have, that no one may take your crown. "He who overcomes, I will make him a pillar in the temple of My God, and he shall go out no more. And I will write on him the name of My God and the name of the city of My God, the New Jerusalem, which comes down out of heaven from My God. And I will write on him My new name. "He who has an ear, let him hear what the Spirit says to the churches."* Rev 3:8—13. The message to the church in Laodicea (Rev 3:14—22) also has many similar characteristics to the current generation. I highly recommend the reader read it.

These prophesied catastrophes in the book of Revelation have been in the Bible for thousands of years. But just as it was at the first coming, the world is preoccupied with modern idols—money, status, business, education, sex, recreation, drugs, and materialism. Spiritually blind Jewish scholars in the past, were jealous and refused to recognize Jesus. Also, in the future, spiritual neglect and spiritual blindness will predominate and prevent rank-and-file Christians, and even Christian scholars, from discerning Him from the Antichrist. Again, beware of the dangers of spiritual neglect which leads to spiritual blindness. True spirituality is essential. The Jewish leadership, at the time of Christ, refused to acknowledge abundant evidence proving Jesus was the Messiah. Listen! If you doubt me please obtain a copy of "**_100 PROPHECIES FULFILLED BY JESUS,_**" by Rose Publishing. I repeat, the Jewish leadership were incapable of recognizing the first visit of Messiah. "He came to His own, and His own did not receive Him. But as many as received Him, to them He gave the right to become children of God, even to those who believe in His name; who were born, not of blood, nor of the will of the flesh, nor of the will of man, but of God. And the Word became flesh and dwelt among us, and we beheld His glory, the glory as of the only begotten of the Father, full of grace and truth." John 1:11—14.

The satanic FRS, described in Revelation 17 as; the great harlot, "the woman was arrayed in purple and scarlet, and adorned with gold and precious stones and pearls, having in her hand a golden cup full of abominations and the filthiness of her fornication. And on her forehead a name was written: **_MYSTERY, BABYLON THE GREAT, THE MOTHER OF HARLOTS AND OF THE ABOMINATIONS OF THE EARTH._**" The False Prophet and the Antichrist will wholeheartedly promote mass deception via this religious monstrosity. Relevant scriptures include these.

"But even if our gospel is veiled, it is veiled to those
who are perishing, whose minds the god of this age

has blinded, who do not believe, lest the light of the gospel of the glory of Christ, who is the image of God, should shine on them". (2 Corinthians 4:3–4)

"Unlike Moses, who put a veil over his face so that the children of Israel could not look steadily at the end of what was passing away. But their minds were hardened. For until this day the same veil remains UNLIFTED in the reading of the Old Testament, because the veil is taken away in Christ. But even to this day, when Moses is read, a veil lies on their heart. Nevertheless when one turns to the Lord, the veil is taken away. Now the Lord is the Spirit; and where the Spirit of the Lord is, there is liberty." (2 Corinthians 3:13–17).

Good news for future Jewish believers in Christ is in Romans 11:25–33.

"For I do not desire, brethren, that you should be ignorant of this mystery, lest you should be wise in your own opinion, that hardening in part has happened to Israel until the fullness of the Gentiles has come in. And so all Israel will be saved, as it is written: "The Deliverer will come out of Zion, And He will turn away ungodliness from Jacob; For this is My covenant with them, When I take away their sins." Concerning the gospel they are enemies for your sake, but concerning the election they are beloved for the sake of the fathers. For the gifts and the calling of God are irrevocable. For as you were once disobedient to God, yet have now obtained mercy through their disobedience, even so these also have now been disobedient, that through the mercy shown you they also may obtain mercy. For God has committed them all to disobedience, that He might have mercy on all. Oh, the depth of the riches both of the wisdom and knowledge of God! How unsearchable are His judgments and His ways past finding out!"

In Revelation 8:12–13, we read,

"Then the fourth angel sounded: and a third of the sun was struck, a third of the moon, and a third of the stars, so that a third of them were darkened; and a third of the day did not shine, and likewise the night. And I looked, and I heard an angel flying through the midst of heaven, saying with a loud voice, "Woe, woe, woe to the inhabitants of the earth, because of the remaining blasts of the trumpet of the three angels who are about to sound."

A couple of observations here. When you were a child, did anyone ever yell at you, "You're gonna get it now!"? That is what this angel was saying to the people; "Woe, woe, woe" indicates severe discipline is coming. What does an angel flying in heaven sound like? Have you ever spooked a bunch of birds? The sound of feathers is distinct. Angel wings are no doubt majestic.

I have never forgotten the words of a prophesy teacher regarding this passage of scripture. I believe it was Dr. Jack Van Impe who said that the dust, ash, and smoke from the previous catastrophes including meteor, asteroid, or comet impacts, nuclear war, cities on fire, movements of earth's tectonic plates resulting in increased earthquakes, and volcanic eruptions would foul the air so much that it would decrease sunlight by a third. Of course, the moon reflects only sunlight. Remember, Father God has finally vented

His wrath after hundreds and thousands of years of grace during the Church Age.

Currently, the warnings of Bible prophesy are considered foolishness. Modern sophisticates scoff and mock at anything biblical. Believers are ridiculed, persecuted and, in certain Islamic countries, slaughtered. Therefore, Father God protects His family via the Rapture. This way, He can more precisely deal with hardened sinners. Reprobates have no idea who they are messing with!

God bless all my mentors. The list includes; Billy Graham, Jerry Falwell, Jack Van Impe, Noah W. Hutchings, Kenneth E. Hagin, Chuck Smith, Hal Lindsey, Grant R. Jeffrey, John Hagee, Perry Stone, David Jeremiah, and many others. Many of them have transitioned to the other side. Van Impe and Lindsey are very elderly now. They continue to preach and teach in spite of the ravages of age and satanic attacks. Like the apostle Paul, they strive to finish strong.

Next, the demons of hell are literally loosed on earth. If you are not safe via salvation, what in heaven's name are you waiting for? You say, "I'm a naturalist and realist." Really? You believe in gravity, electricity, and subatomic particles. These are rational constructs that cannot be seen by the human eye, but we know they exist. Christ compared the spirit realm to the wind; you can't see the wind, but you can see its effects. Even so, when salvation, healing, or demonic deliverance takes place, that is the visible evidence of the spirit realm. Outright miracles still occur. Missionaries attest to this. In modern America, the **700 Club** TV program has many documented miracles. Learning to discern spiritually during our earthly life helps prepare us for the next stage of our development.

Please read Revelation Chapter 9; I am going to refer to it often. The star fallen from heaven to the earth, could be the death angel referred to earlier. In verse 11, this angel is identified as "the angel of the bottomless pit, whose name in Hebrew is Abaddon, but in Greek he has the name Apollyon." (Rev 9:11) Both names mean "destruction" as per the *Ryrie Study Bible,* page 1798. The locusts are demonic creatures; they are not called angels.

> "The shape of the locusts was like horses prepared for battle; and on their heads were crowns of something like gold, and their faces were like the faces of men. They had hair like women's hair, and their teeth were like lions' teeth. And they had breastplates of iron, and the sound of their wings was like the sound of chariots with many horses running into battle. They had tails like scorpions, and there were stings in their tails. And their power was to hurt men five months." Rev 9:7—10.

Again, even Stephen Spielberg would be challenged to replicate these creatures. Okay, quite a few symbols here. Before I give my musings, what do *you* think these symbols are meant to convey?

Symbols and Terms Followed by Suggested Interpretations

- locusts—plagues from God and imply a large powerful army about to invade (Tanks?)
- horses prepared for battle—imminent warfare (Personnel carriers?)
- crowns—godly authority, combat excellence
- faces of men—intended for humankind, designed for human punishment (Soldiers?)
- women's hair—neglected, untamed, barbaric (Rebellious, offensive?)
- lion's teeth—danger and intimidation, lethal (Brutal, vicious)
- breastplates of iron—strong, battle ready (Body Armor?)

- chariots with many horses running into battle—violent, overwhelming force (Tanks, Trucks, Armored vehicles)
- scorpion stings—evil, cursed, painful (Guns, cannons, artillery, smart missiles)

These powerful creatures are tools God uses to punish rebellious humankind. They have been held in restraint for thousands of years, until grace and mercy are exhausted, then mocked. Their bizarre appearance is not atypical of God. Compare the world of insects or deep-sea creatures. Consider the violence in nature, including insects and animals. What a nightmare for the ungodly. Millions of moviegoers delight in horror and graphic violence, but this is **REAL** . These terrible plagues could happen to you, if you reject our Redeemer and Savior.

Are you a closet atheist? Do you consider prophesy as science fiction? However, deep down, are you bothered by existential uncertainties? Common sense rejects a random, impersonal universe; there has to be a reason for our existence. Some of our greatest minds were Christians—Francis Bacon, Copernicus, Pascal, Isaac Newton, Johannes Kepler, and more recently Wernher von Braun. Today, many scientists and Medical Doctors are Christians. Most if not all of our Founding Fathers were godly men—George Washington, John Adams, John Quincy Adams, Benjamin Franklin, John Hancock, Patrick Henry, Thomas Jefferson, and many others. These men were visionaries. They were not ashamed of God. I recommend two books by highly educated Christian scientists: *Many Infallible Proofs* by Dr's Henry Morris and Henry Morris III and *God of the Big Bang* by Dr. Leslie Wickman.

All Seekers of God, Accept Christ as Your Lord and Savior

1. Admit you are a sinner.
2. Agree with God and turn (repent) from known sin.

3. By faith, believe that Jesus suffered and died to pay for your sins.
4. Prayerfully invite Jesus into your heart as your Lord and Savior.

Prayer

Dear God, I believe that your Son, Jesus, suffered and died on the cross to pay for my sins. Through faith in Christ, I accept Jesus as my Lord and Savior. Thank you for forgiving me and cleansing me from all sin. Help me to live for you and depend on you all the days of my life, amen.

The bizarre locusts in chapter 9 came out of the bottomless pit. The angel in charge of the bottomless pit is given a Hebrew name, Abaddon, and a Greek name, Apollyon. Both names mean "destruction." No one knows the location of the bottomless pit, but some indications suggest it is deep in the earth (Philippians 2:10). These creatures were given specific orders as to what they could and could not do. Notice that even Satan and the demons do not dare exceed their instructions. Yet humankind, even with extensive history records, is once again unwilling to respect the God of the Bible.

Next, John's powerful vision directs us to the sixth angel with the sixth trumpet judgment. This angel was instructed by a voice from the four horns of the golden altar saying, "Release the four angels who are bound at the great River Euphrates" (Revelation 9:14). The Euphrates runs through Syria and Iraq, both of which were part of the old Persian Empire. It is no coincidence that Syria, Iraq, and Iran are almost daily in the news. Could it be that World War III is triggered from this region?

Verse 15 reveals that these four angels had been prepared specifically "for the hour and day and month and year, were released to kill a third of mankind." Just another example of the foreknowledge and precision of our Creator. It may take thousands of years, but God always does what He says He will do. Brethren, sometimes the delay between sin and punishment causes us to think that God is not watching, or worse that He does not exist. It annoyed King David and many others, including myself, that evil people *seem* to get away with sin, a dynamic described in Psalm 73. However, nothing gets by our God: "Do not be deceived, God is not mocked; for what ever a man sows, that he will also reap" (Galatians 6:7).

These four angels were assigned to kill a third of evil humankind. Scripture describes an army of two hundred million horsemen. Some Bible scholars feel these horsemen are symbolic of tanks or other mechanized armor. That is possible, but they could also be demonic creatures. Only Father God knows for sure. Can you see why many preachers shy away from teaching Revelation, with all of its bizarre symbols?

Is there any significance to the three colors—red, blue, and yellow—in verse 17? Is it just a coincidence that the flags of the Russian Federation ground forces is red and yellow! Also, red and yellow are the colors of the People's Republic of China, according to Wikipedia? The Chinese ensign of the People's Liberation Army *Air Force* is red, yellow, and blue (Wikipedia). There is more; "Nader Shah was one of the most powerful Iranian rulers in the history of the nation, ruling as Shah of Iran (Persia) from 1736 to 1747" (Wikipedia). His royal flag was red and yellow with a lion in the center (Wikipedia).

Scripture is clear that this army of 200 million with "breastplates of fiery red, hyacinth blue, and sulfur yellow" kills a third of humankind. Any coincidence that Ezekiel 38 and the battle of Armageddon mention Russia and Persia and the kings of the east? The Ezekiel 38 war *prominently* mentions Russia and Persia. The final war of Armageddon includes the kings of the east (Revelation 16:12). According to the *Ryrie Study Bible* (page 1806) and other sources, the kings of the east are "the kings of the rising sun. The armies of the nations of the Orient will be aided in their march toward Armageddon by the Supernatural drying up of the Euphrates River."

China has only recently developed into a major world power. A third of humankind was killed by the fire, smoke, and brimstone that came out of their mouths (Revelation 9:18). Sounds like global warfare to me.

According to my sources, Brimstone refers to sulfur. "This may also refer to lava or falling ash from a volcanic eruption that would emit suffocating sulfurous gases especially sulfur dioxide. The nauseous odor of brimstone pervaded the atmosphere and tarnished brass on ships in the area for weeks after the volcanic destruction of Krakatoa in 1883."

> "The word "brimstone" occurs 14 times in the Bible and is used in every instance to indicate punishment and devastation for sin, probably because of its brilliant flame. Evil men and their land would be covered with brimstone (Deut 29:23; Ezekiel 38:22; Job 18:15; Psalm 11:6). In the day of god's vengeance His breath would become as brimstone (Isa 30:33), as would the dust (Isa 34:9). Sodom (q.v.) and Gomorrah were thus destroyed (Genesis 19:24; Lk 17:29). John saw idolaters and those who worshiped the Beast destroyed by fire and brimstone (Rev 9:17–18; 14:10; 19:20). The devil and the wicked will be cast into the lake of fire and brimstone"(Rev 21:8; 20:10). (*Wycliffe Bible Dictionary*, 1123)

Can you believe that the survivors of these plagues refused to repent and turn to God? (Revelation 9:20). They are like cancer cells. They have one agenda—replicate and consume the host victim. The only remedy is to surgically remove them before it is too late. Spiritually, they are reprobates committed to their ungodly agendas. They have no intention of submitting to a holy God.

Let us look at the sins of the generation that will exist during the great tribulation period. I see similarities to current news reports. Apostasy in America and the world has resulted in nightly shootings, murders, rapes, molestations, home invasions, thefts, business and government corruption, fraud, bribery, embezzlement, cybercrime, money laundering, identity theft, and forgery. Man without God is an animal.

I bring your attention to two specific sins—idol worship and sorcery. Some say that those kind of sins do not occur in our society, but they do! Our so-called modern, sophisticated society is currently preoccupied with idols such as money, materialism, career, recreation, sex, alcohol and drugs, status, and power, whether physical, financial, or legal. In the near future, the masses will deliberately worship demons and interact with an idol, specifically, the Robot image of the 'World Leader' (much more on the image of the beast when we get to Revelation 13).

Regarding sorcery, millions are addicted to drugs and alcohol. Sorcery includes illicit spiritualism and the abuse of drugs and alcohol. Some play with witchcraft while others practice it. Witchcraft, occult-based video games, and science fiction are very popular. Satan uses these as bait to capture those who participate in witchcraft, psychic phenomena, fortune-telling, new-age mediums, spirit channeling, and the like. I believe any participation in, and preoccupation with witchcraft, drugs, alcohol, and illicit sex can open the door for demons. I do not claim to understand it all. However, once a demonic stronghold is formed, it is a battle to get free of its control and afflictions. I believe Satan is laughing as many Americans are voting for recreational use of marijuana. Common sense tells us what this will lead to. There is documented evidence that marijuana can lead to mental illness and violence (2). We should be seeking to be filled with the Holy Spirit, not seeking to get high on alcohol or drugs (Ephesians 5:18).

CHAPTER 4
Revelation 10–11

Revelation chapter 10 contains a description of a 'mighty angel' that seems to have God-like attributes. Is this 'mighty angel' Jesus? Compare this mighty angel with Revelation 1:13–18, Ezekiel 1:26–28 and 43:1–4, and Daniel 7:9–10. Could it be Jesus? Only Father God knows.

Jesus made several post-crucifixion appearances that were initially misidentified (John 20:15; Luke 24:13–31). Since "no prophesy of scripture is of any private interpretation" (2 Peter 1:20), no human can claim infallibility. Perhaps this mighty angel of Revelation 10:1 is a theophanic angel, "a manifestation of God to man, either in human or symbolic form in order to impart God's will to that person" (*Wycliffe Bible Dictionary*, 1696). This brief portion of the definition does not include the total information about a theophany. I agree with the *HCSB Study Bible* regarding Revelation 10:1.

> The mighty angel could be: (1) the angel introduced in 5:2, (2) the angel seen in 18:1, or (3) another angel altogether. In spite of his impressive appearance and the similarity to the vision of the Son of Man (i.e., the glorified Christ) in 1:13–16, it is unlikely this is Christ. Christ is never called an angel elsewhere in the NT. (*HCSB Study Bible*, 2212).

Let us move on with Chapter 10. First, let us look at the little book and the seven thunders. I suspect the little book and the seven thunders contain privileged, top-secret information. I have an idea why Father God chose not to reveal this information—just speculation on my part. This sealed information may pertain to the satanic trinity and the initiation of the Kingdom Age. Of course the satanic trinity comprises Satan, the Antichrist, and the False Prophet. Satan would just love to plan his schemes according to the revealed will of God, but the hidden things belong to God and to those He chooses to reveal them (Deuteronomy 29:29; Matthew 13:11–13).

This sealed, secret information reminds me of the 1983 movie *Sudden Impact* with Clint Eastwood. Toward the end of the movie, Eastwood says to the bad guy, "Go ahead. Make my day." The bad guy did not know if Eastwood was out of ammunition, would back down, or would blow him away with his impressive .44 Magnum. In a similar manner, Satan must make his move not knowing how God will react. Father God is sovereign, and so are His mysteries (1 Corinthians 4:1).

Revelation 10:5–7 declares that a major transition is taking place.

> "And the angel whom I saw standing on the sea and on the land, lifted up his hand to heaven and swore by Him who lives forever and ever, who created HEAVEN and the things that are in it, the EARTH and the things that are in it, and the SEA and the things that are in it, that there should be delay no longer, but in the days of the sounding of the seventh angel, when he is about to sound, THE MYSTERY OF GOD would be FINISHED, as He declared to His servants the prophets."

Father God's patience with humankind and Satan is about over. These verses describe God almighty retaking delegated authority from Satan. This mighty angel with many attributes of God is seen standing with his right foot on the sea and his left foot on the land, showing total ownership. This mighty angel reaffirms that God Himself (Jesus) created "heaven and the things that are in it, the earth and the things that are in it, and the sea and the things that are in it." Satan is thoroughly dispossessed. Regarding verses 8–11, while the Word of God is always good, the reality and effect of these prophetic scriptures are bitter.

Chapter 11 contains an abundance of issues and topics; no doubt an entire book could be written about it. If anyone has ever wondered if the Jews will rebuild their temple, chapter 11 answers in the affirmative. But the 'Dome of the Rock', which may reside on the court outside the temple, is not to be measured. The Antichrist has temporarily patched an uneasy coexistence between Gentiles and Jews. Remember, many Jews have yet to recognize Jesus as the Messiah. The masses, whether Gentiles or Jews, have been deceived and accepted the Antichrist as Messiah. As prophesy has foretold, this generation is not only deceived, but as corrupt as in the days of Noah and Lot.

The ***true church*** is gone, having finished its mission. The faithful believers have been 'beamed up' via the Rapture. Though messianic Jews and Christians have been removed for their protection, Father God will always provide individuals such as the 144,000 Jewish witnesses to preach the gospel message. Just as Noah preached the truth during his wicked generation and Lot preached the truth in his wicked generation, God will always have His witness and voice in every generation.

> "Then I was given a reed like a measuring rod. And the angel stood, saying, "Rise and measure the temple of God, the altar, and those who worship there. "But leave out the court which is outside the temple, and do not measure it, for it has been given to the Gentiles. And they will tread the holy

city underfoot for forty two months." (Revelation 11:1–2)

Whenever measuring is going on, it almost always means construction. Here, it indicates construction of the end-time temple.

> "And I will give power to My two witnesses, and they will prophesy one thousand two hundred and 60 days, clothed in sackcloth. These are the two olive trees and the two lampstands standing before the God of the earth." (Revelation 11:3–4)

Here, God identifies His two chosen witnesses for this time, which is during the seven-year tribulation period. Remember that three and a half, plus three and a half, equals seven, a number attributed to God as it denotes perfection and completion.

In my humble opinion, the two witnesses are Moses and Elijah. I have debated and discussed this issue many times. Everybody is entitled to his or her opinion. We will find out for sure when we get to the other side.

They are clothed in sackcloth because of the sorry, sordid, and sinful situation going on with humankind, the Antichrist and the False Religious System (FRS). Specifically, active worship of a false messiah, demons, and a thriving apostate church.

> "Then the Lord saw that the wickedness of man was GREAT in the earth, and that EVERY intent of the thoughts of his heart was only EVIL CONTINUALLY. And the Lord was sorry that He had made man on the earth, and He was GRIEVED in His heart." (Genesis 6:5–6)

Once again, we have broken God's heart. He wants to bless us and take care of us, but He will not violate His standards.

> "O Jerusalem, Jerusalem, the one who kills the
> prophets and stones those who are sent to her! How
> often I wanted to gather your children together, as
> a hen gathers her chicks under her wings, but you
> were not willing! ... See! Your house is left to you
> desolate; for I say to you, you shall see me no more
> till you say, "Blessed is He who comes in the name
> of the Lord!" (Matthew 23:37–39)

Moving on, let us discuss the 'two witnesses'. Talk about a hostile crowd. Talk about a tough assignment, the two witnesses are called to preach to "the cowardly, unbelieving, abominable, murderers, sexually immoral, sorcerers, idolaters, and all liars" (Revelation 21:8). Imagine the typical, modern, sophisticated crowd full of pride and indignation toward anyone who dared disagree with their 'great leader', the Antichrist. This generation vehemently denies the concepts of truth and moral absolutes. Yet they had to respect these two men because "if anyone wants to harm them, fire proceeds from their mouth and devours their enemies" (v. 5). Common sense says that if these men had supernatural power and said they were sent from God, it would be a good idea to investigate and listen to them. But just like today, wicked men have made up their minds and ignore ideas not accepted by the 'elite'. They are sycophants, and refuse to think for themselves. The cowardly would not think of resisting the current consensus or zeitgeist. The proud are not interested in truth and do not want to reason. They do not care about right or wrong because to them, there is no right or wrong.

No doubt these two prophets were exposing the Antichrist as a fraud and preaching Jesus as the true Messiah. These two preachers, or witnesses, will be ridiculed by hordes of reprobates, but they cannot be ignored. These anointed men of God are given power to withhold rain and to "strike the earth with all plagues, as often as they desire" (Revelation 11:6). Did these mighty miracles have any effect on this evil end time generation? When Father

God has finished using the two witnesses (Moses and Elijah), only then will the Antichrist be allowed to kill them. Yet just as in the murder of Jesus, Father God shows up and demonstrates who has the **REAL POWER.**

> "Then those from the peoples, tribes, tongues, and nations will SEE their dead bodies three and a half days, and not allow their dead bodies to be put into graves. And those who dwell on the earth will rejoice over them, make merry, and send gifts to one another, because these two prophets tormented those who dwell on the earth. Now after the three and a half days the breath of life from God entered them, and they stood on their feet, and great fear fell on those who saw them. And they heard a loud voice from heaven saying to them, "COME UP HERE." And they ascended to heaven in a cloud, and their enemies SAW them. In the same hour there was a great earthquake, and a tenth of the city fell. In the earthquake seven thousand men were killed, and the rest were afraid and gave glory to the God of heaven." (Revelation 11:9–13)

Only God has power over death. Amazingly, some of these end-time people finally became "afraid and gave glory to the God of heaven."

Allow me to present another important implication of the above scriptures. I believe it was Pastor John Hagee who directed my attention to an important aspect of technology and Bible prophesy. The following quote is a powerful indication that the second coming of Christ could be near. I quote from my first book, *Mr. President, I Respectfully Disagree*, pages 24–25).

> "I want to bring your attention to specific verses: Revelation 11:9, 11, and 12. Verse 9 says, "Then

those from the peoples, tribes, tongues, and nations will SEE their dead bodies." Verse 11: And a great fear fell on those who SAW them." Verse 12: "And their enemies SAW THEM." Before satellite TV and computers, it was IMPOSSIBLE for these prophetic scriptures to play out. This is just one of dozens of indications that end-time prophecies could soon be fulfilled, and reinforce the fact that we could be near the end of the Church Age."

Technology has developed such that a global 'Mark Of The Beast' and 'Image Of The Beast', and a worldwide economic system CAN NOW EXIST. As a matter of fact, signs number two and six in my first book are now possible because of ___recent technological advancements.___ Sign number two in my first book was; The Explosion of Technology, Travel and Knowledge within the last one hundred years (Daniel 12:4). Sign number Six; Worldwide Evangelism. (Matthew 24:14)

Brethren, I have identified three 'signs' or 'birth pangs' that I call **SUPER SIGNS.** These three super signs confirm and reinforce that we are near the greatest event of history. See if you agree; Sign #1. The rebirth of Israel as a nation (Matt 24:32. Sign #2. The *convergence* of multiple birth pangs and signs at the same time (Matt 24:33,34). Sign #3. World Wide Evangelism (Matt 24:14).

As Bishop T. D. Jakes says ..."get ready, get ready, get ready." As Pastor John Hagee says ..." Christ can come before your next breath!"

All Seekers of God, Accept Christ as Your Lord and Savior

1. Admit you are a sinner.
2. Agree with God and turn (repent) from known sin.

3. By faith, believe that Jesus suffered and died to pay for your sins.

4. Prayerfully invite Jesus into your heart as your Lord and Savior.

Prayer

Dear God, I believe that your Son, Jesus, suffered and died on the cross to pay for my sins. Through faith in Christ, I accept Jesus as my Lord and Savior. Thank you for forgiving me and cleansing me from all sin. Help me to live for you and depend on you all the days of my life, amen.

Please allow a little repetition as we return to Revelation 11:13. The same hour that the citizens of Jerusalem and the citizens of the world (via satellite) saw the two witnesses become alive and ascend into the clouds of heaven, a great earthquake occurred. Seven thousand men were killed. Trauma after trauma finally shook some sense into the survivors; "The rest were afraid and gave glory to the God of heaven" (Revelation 11:13). This reminds me of the Roman centurion who after witnessing the crucifixion of Christ, the solar eclipse, and Jesus crying out to the Father, said, "Truly this man was the Son of God!" (Mark 15:39).

Brethren, does God have to turn off the sun (eclipse) and shake the ground (earthquake) to get your attention? As stated previously, modern technology has made possible the fulfillment of Bible prophesies that seemed impossible for thousands of years. The birth of the nation of Israel in 1948 was thought impossible. Advances in mathematics, computers, communications, and satellites enable financial institutions to handle global accounting tasks, such as the "Mark Of The Beast". You better believe the coming Antichrist will make use of surveillance technology to control buying and selling during his evil reign. If you think the ***convergence*** of modern technology and bible prophesy is just a coincidence, I have some oceanfront property in Kansas to sell you!

In Revelation 11:15, we read that humankind has struggled for thousands of years with the consequences of the fall. Finally, we see the actual transfer of delegated authority from "the god of this world" (KJV), Satan (2 Corinthians 4:4), back to the kingdom of God. Finally, Father God lifts the curse. We no longer have to pray, "Thy kingdom come" (Matthew 6:10). The lesson about trusting in nonbiblical sources should be clear. Since the fall, Father God allows humankind to choose. Will it be the God of the Bible, or, politically correct academia, news media, and liberal theologians? Listen! Father God's plan for the ages is almost over. Your words and deeds reveal who you are. Those who have made godly choices by faith, are blessed, so it's time for the final exam.

> "The court was seated, And the books were opened … And I saw the dead, small and great, standing before God, and books were opened. And another book was opened, which is the Book of Life. And the dead were judged according to their works, by the things which were written in the books." (Daniel 7:10; Revelation 20:12)

Father God has done everything, including sending His Son to *die for us* as a sacrifice to provide atonement for our sins.

> "the dispensation of the grace of God … how that by revelation He made known to me the mystery … which in other ages was not made known to the sons of men, as it has now been revealed by the Spirit to His holy apostles and prophets: that the Gentiles should be fellow heirs, of the same body, and partakers of His promise in Christ through the gospel … and to make ALL people see what

is the fellowship of the mystery, which from the beginning of the ages has been hidden in God who created all things through Jesus Christ; to the intent now the manifold wisdom of God might be made known BY THE CHURCH to the principalities and powers in the heavenly places, according to the eternal purpose which He accomplished in Christ Jesus our Lord, in whom we have boldness and access with confidence through FAITH IN HIM." (Ephesians 3:2, 3, 5, 6, 9–12)

Father God loves all—Jew and Gentile alike. The offer of salvation is to "whosoever" (John 3:16). Generation after generation now knows the benefits of trusting in Christ and the dangers and curses of trusting in ***self and non biblical sources.*** Revelation chapter 11 reports that Kingdom Age benefits are imminent. This reminds me of what Dr. Martin Luther King said, "Free at last, Free at last, thank God Almighty, free at last !"

Finally, The twenty-four elders' song of praise in verses 17–18 sums up the events that are about to take place. I count at least four.

1. thanksgiving for finally taking back authority from Satan over the earth
2. thanks for judging and punishing evil
3. thanks for rewarding faithful believers
4. thanks for punishing those who have abused and polluted the earth

Chapter 5
Revelation 12–14

If you do not like symbols, parables, and allegories, you might have a difficult time with chapter 12. But fear not; let us boldly trust God in all things because 'spiritual dream language' can be demystified and clarified. If Father God did not want us to seek understanding, He would not have made it cryptic and dreamlike. By faith, ask, seek, and knock.

Persistence and determination are life lessons I had to learn repeatedly. This book is a good example. You better believe that Satan tried to discourage me throughout the process. Headaches, computer problems, printer problems, family distractions, were often deterrents I had to deal with. In my youth and early adult years, I gave up to easily. Learning to ride a bicycle, and learning to type, both took time and determination. Writing a book, especially a Christian book, requires titantic persistence. Parents, teach your children perseverance. It is one of the principals of success, whether physical, mental or social.

I believe that Father God deliberately made Revelation cryptic to pique our interest. Most people enjoy a good treasure hunt. But, don't give up to easy. Learning to discern the voice of God takes time and effort. Not that I have learned everything there is to learn. Often, when I am desperate and determined, **that** is when the solution comes to me. Thank you, Lord, for opening our eyes as we seek understanding of scriptures, or any prayer request.

Topics, issues, and items for this chapter include; a woman clothed with the sun, the moon under her feet, a garland of twelve stars, pain of childbirth, a great, fiery-red dragon with seven heads and ten horns, a third of the stars thrown to the earth, her child caught up to God and His throne, war breaking out in heaven, Satan being cast down to the earth, the blood of the Lamb, the word of their testimony, their self-denial and death to self, persecution of the woman, and the dragon being enraged with the woman and making war on the rest of her offspring.

I'll give you a short and skinny interpretation of chapter 12, based on my meditation (focused seeking), and best guesses. The woman in 12:1 is probably the nation of Israel. The male child is Jesus. Of course, the dragon, serpent, and devil are the same person—Satan. The third of the stars of heaven thrown to the earth are *fallen angels* who follow Satan. Notice two of the main activities of Satan—*deceiving* (Rev 12:9) and *accusing* (Rev 12:10). If you follow politics as I do, you know that Satan is very active with lying, accusing and deceiving (LAD). In every generation he is behind the scenes. I hope you will pray for our leaders, and seek godly discernment. Because Satan is alive and active in every generation.

The 'child' is none other than Jesus, who was resurrected and ascended to God's throne. Again, the woman is the nation of Israel that had to flee into the wilderness and was protected by God. At this time, war broke out in heaven. Satan and his angels were roughed up, beaten up, humiliated, and cast to the earth. The residents of heaven rejoice because this troublemaker has finally been cast out of heaven. But woe to people of earth, "for the devil has come down to you, having great wrath, because he knows that he has a short time" (Revelation 12:12). Is this why there has been a tremendous increase in division and malice at every level of society? Has Satan been cast to our earth? Even though a dragon is scary (Ha!), even a child who believes in Christ can send him fleeing (James 4:6–8). Spiritual warfare is real, and every child of God needs to learn how to deal with the forces of evil.

Please notice important strategies of spiritual warfare in verse 11: "And they overcame him (Satan) by the blood of the Lamb, (salvation) and by the word of their testimony (professions, declarations, and lifestyle), and they did not love their lives to the death (self denial)." That is, they accepted Christ as Lord and Savior, they spoke and lived by faith, and they died to their own desires to the extent of martyrdom if necessary. Remember, "Without FAITH it is impossible to please Him" (Hebrews 11:6). "For whatever is born of God overcomes the world. And this is the victory that has overcome the world—our FAITH. Who is he who overcomes the world, but he who believes that Jesus is the Son of God" (1 John 5:4–5). Two very important spiritual weapons are; the 'shield of faith', and the 'sword of the Spirit, which is the word of God' Eph 6:11—18.

Faith must be in harmony with God's will, not name it and claim it. Our motives must be pure. Selfishness instantly short-circuits our prayers. Our faith and prayers can be hindered by unconfessed sin, doubt and unbelief, and mistreatment of others. Successful faith-filled prayer includes a desire to live a godly life and forsaking any known sin. Successful prayer often includes persistent, earnest and fervent petitions (James 5:15–18; Luke 11:5–13; I'm preaching to myself here).

Verse 17 of chapter 12 presents a question—are the offspring (children) of the woman, (Israel); are they Jews or Christians? I believe both. It seems to me that those "who keep the commandments of God **AND** have the testimony of Jesus Christ" includes Jews, messianic Jews, and Christians.

> "For the Scripture says, "Whoever believes on Him will not be put to shame." For there is no distinction between Jew and Greek, for the same Lord over all is rich to all who call upon Him. For "whoever calls upon the name of the Lord shall be saved." (Romans 10:11–13; see also John 3:16)

Satan is enraged with anyone who dares follow scripture and accepts Christ as his or her Savior. He is an evil adversary who is 'good' at what he does. He would love to strike back at God, but the best he can do is try to steal, kill, and destroy God's favorite creation— humankind. He can't even do that if the intended victim persists in spiritual warfare, regardless of the storms of life. (See the book of Job)

The woman, Israel, was given 'two wings of a great eagle'; the 'two wings of a great eagle' could symbolize God, or aircraft from nations sympathetic toward the persecuted Jews: "I bore you on eagles wings and brought you to Myself" (Exodus 19:4). Scripture is replete with occasions where Father God intervened and protected Jews and Christians. Satan has tried many times to destroy Jews and Christians. But invariably, even displacement and dispersion resulted in spread of the faith. Father God knows how to create and maintain safe havens all over the world. When Pharaoh tried to subjugate and slaughter Jews, his army became fish food. When England persecuted and limited Christians, they (Puritans / Pilgrims) left all and boarded the Mayflower. They sailed to North America. The rest is history, as they say.

When the Jews sinned, God allowed their enemies to rule over them—for a time. Babylon succeeded —for a time. Rome succeeded —for a time. Herod tried to kill Christ, as a toddler. Nero greatly persecuted the Christians —for a time. Islam has a history of persecution and slaughter of Jews and Christians alike. Hitler greatly persecuted and slaughtered Jews —for a time. Mostly Christian nations gradually destroyed Hitler and the Nazi war machine. Now, secular humanism, the ACLU, atheists, progressives and democrats, the Obama administration, the US Supreme Court, much of academia, and the politically correct crowd, are partially succeeding —for a time.

The Jews are back in Israel and constitute a very strong country. The Christian church is down but not out. Christian law firms are winning legal attacks. Christianity is prospering in selected countries and cities. How does Satan feel about all that? "And the dragon was ENRAGED with the woman, and he went to make war with the rest of her offspring, who keep the commandments of God AND have the testimony of Jesus Christ" (Revelation 12:17). Do you really think at this stage in the cosmic conflict, Father God would abandon his chosen people, both Jews and Gentiles? Revelation, the last book of the Bible, tells us how it all plays out. Why not get on the winning team?

Revelation 13 contains many more symbols. By the way, the number 'thirteen' in Bible numerology represents sin, rebellion, apostasy and depravity according to my sources (1).

Scripture is full of cryptic symbols, parables, clues, and metaphors. Often, they are difficult to understand, until after the event or prophesy has occurred. But if Father God is approached and petitioned in the proper way, He may or may not reveal His will to the seeker. "Surely the Lord God does nothing, Unless He reveals His secret to His servants the prophets" (Amos 3:7). Prophets were active even in the early church (Acts 11:27, 21:10–12). There is a difference between the office of a prophet in the Old Testament and the spiritual gift of prophecy in the New Testament. The New Testament tells us, "But he who prophesies speaks edification and exhortation and comfort to men" (1 Corinthians 14:3).

Brethren, let us continue to ask God to open our eyes to decipher and understand His allegorical language. I believe He absolutely wants to blow our minds with fulfilled prophesy. Why? Because it verifies He is truly God, and, only **_GOD_** knows the future. Fulfilled prophesy is one of "many infallible proofs" (Acts 1:3). (For more information regarding infallible proofs, read *Many Infallible Proofs* by Dr's Henry Morris and Henry Morris III.)

Before I launch into chapter 13, I would like to present a poem about the Antichrist.

"The Pompous Little Man"

I am a pompous little man
Don't tell me what to do!
Only I say what <u>you</u> can do

Simple people need a leader
A great man, strong as cedar
But they don't know I am a cheater

People are stupid!
I know what they did
From me they cannot be hid
From me they will be rid

He is a pompous little man,
So said the Prophet Dan
"Who, me? In God's frying pan"!

There is a cornucopia of topics, issues, and symbols in chapter 13. These include a beast rising out of the <u>sea</u>, seven heads and ten horns, a leopard, a bear, and a lion. Also, 'saints led into captivity, saints killed with the sword'. Numerous additional symbols; "another beast coming up out of the <u>earth</u>, and he had two horns like a lamb and spoke like a dragon" Rev 13:11. Also, 'dragon and beast worship, a deadly wound being healed, great signs and wonders, the image (idol) of the beast, worship of the image; and 'mark, name, and number of the beast'. The Antichrist's number is 666. The Antichrist's system of government is socialism on steroids! Every word and deed is monitored and tracked by sophisticated surveillance technology. To disagree is considered 'defective or disloyal'. Does this sound familiar?

The beast from the <u>sea</u> is the **political** Antichrist. The seven heads could represent the Antichrist's global empire, perhaps one head for each continent or one for each of the seven wealthiest countries. The ten horns could represent the ten most powerful nations that give their allegiance to the Antichrist. Each head and horn is given over to satanic forces, so this beast's government is a combination of wealth and military power. The phrase "like a leopard" could refer to the Greek Empire under Alexander the Great (2). The phrase "A bear" could refer to the Medo-Persian Empire (3). "A lion" with eagle's wings could refer to the Babylonian Empire (4). So this end-time beast government is a combination of the best features of past world empires. This is none other than the much sought after **_Revived Roman Empire_** . It is the final manifestation of Rome, namely, the kingdom represented by the legs of iron and feet, 'partly of clay and partly of iron' (Daniel 2:41–44). It is Satan's counterfeit kingdom.

Our adversary has tried to achieve control of humankind since the Garden of Eden. You would think that humanity would learn from history, but generation after generation has repeated the same mistakes. This time, worldwide apostasy has resulted in hordes of reprobates. Persistent sin sears the conscience and makes us vulnerable to deception. Satan will exploit this dynamic. This time, Father God allows sinful man to have his way— temporarily. Yet, scripture reveals, when God has had enough, He will intervene.

The prophet Daniel and the apostle John were both directed to use the leopard, bear, and lion as symbols; this is just one of many examples of harmony in the sixty-six books of the Bible. The Bible was written over approximately 1,500 years by more than forty human authors. The Bible's entire message is consistent and cohesive (5). The harmony and consistency of the Bible strongly indicates a solitary author—**_GOD!_** The following URL will guide the reader to an article discussing this phenomena: https://www.christiananswers.net/q-aiia/biblecongruency.html. This is another indication of the divine inspiration of the Bible. In addition to the above, I refer readers to *50 Proofs for the Bible: Old Testament* (pamphlet) and *50 Proofs for the Bible: New Testament* (pamphlet) by

Rose Publishing. Archaeology repeatedly confirms the accuracy of scripture, and prophecy repeatedly confirms the authenticity and divinity of scripture. Brethren, God is **_REAL!_**

"And I saw one of his heads AS IF it had been mortally wounded, and his deadly wound was healed. And all the world MARVELED and followed the beast" (Revelation 13:3). This probably refers to an assassination attempt on the Antichrist; it could occur at the middle of the seven-year tribulation period (Matthew 24:15; Daniel 9:27; 2 Thessalonians 2:4; Revelation 13:14–15). Satan, the great con artist and illusionist, greatly strengthens deception with a false resurrection event. I was thirteen when President Kennedy was assassinated. After watching the film footage (uncensored) of the actual assassination, no one would believe President Kennedy could have survived that head wound.

> So they worshiped the dragon who gave authority to the beast; and they worshiped the beast, saying, "Who is like the beast? Who is able to make war with him?" And he was given a mouth speaking great things and blasphemies, and he WAS GIVEN authority to continue for forty-two months. (Revelation 13:4–5)

Here we see outright worship of Satan and the false messiah or Antichrist. He is considered 'all powerful' by the masses of reprobates. Did you notice that the Antichrist is permitted, or allowed, to speak blasphemies and given authority for forty-two months? He is on a short leash. Worship is what Satan has wanted all along (Isaiah 14:14; Matthew 4:9).

The second beast comes up out of the **_earth_**. He has "two horns like a lamb and spoke like a dragon." This is the False Prophet, who heads up the apostate world religious system or FRS. Both beasts, political and religious—iron and clay—will work in lockstep to promote and require mandatory worship of the political Antichrist.

These two world leaders give full vent to their contempt for Judeo-Christian authority. They are even allowed temporary authority to overcome the tribulation saints. These tribulation saints are not the church; the church was raptured in chapter 4.

> He (False Prophet) performs great signs, so that he even makes fire come down from heaven on the earth in the sight of men. And he deceives those who dwell on the earth by those signs which he was granted to do in the sight of the beast, telling those who dwell on the earth to make an IMAGE to the beast who was wounded by the sword and lived. He was granted power to give BREATH (Artificial Intelligence?) to the IMAGE of the beast, that the IMAGE of the beast should both SPEAK and cause as many as would NOT worship the IMAGE of the beast to be killed. And he causes all, both small and great, rich and poor, free and slave, to receive a MARK on their right hand or on their foreheads, and that no one may BUY OR SELL except one who has the MARK or the NAME of the beast, or the NUMBER of his name. Here is wisdom. Let him who has understanding CALCULATE the NUMBER of the beast, for it is the NUMBER of a man: His number is 666. (Revelation 13:13–18)

Could the three sixes symbolize a maximum union of **_human_** physical, mental, and spiritual development? Six is the number of man. Humanism on steroids. It could also mathematically compute or calculate the name of the Antichrist. The *Wycliffe Bible Dictionary* says the following about the number 666.

> "The only authentic example of a mystical number in the Bible is the number of the name of the Beast,

666 (a variant reading is 616), in Revelation 13:17-18. It is obvious that the apostle John knew it had a hidden meaning, for he wrote, "Here is wisdom. Let him who has understanding calculate the number of the beast, for the number is that of a man, and his number is six hundred and sixty-six" (v 18, NASB). Various interpretations have been suggested. By GEMATRIA the number 666 has been identified with the numerical values of the names of various prominent persons from the Roman emperors Caligula, Nero, and Trajan onward, and with such concepts as the chaos monster. The most probable of the historical personages is Nero(n) Caesar (in Heb. Letters): n-r-w-n q-s-r, 50 + 200 + 6 + 50 + 100 + 60 + 200 = 666. Ed.). (6)

Brethren, there are tons of scriptures that indicate God allows testing and even severe testing. The book of Job is a good example. God's call to Abraham to sacrifice Isaac is an example. Father God did not allow Abraham to actually sacrifice his son, but He did allow cruel Jewish and Roman leaders to crucify His only begotten Son.

The Antichrist, False Prophet, and hordes of reprobate humanity are thoroughly possessed. The 'pillars' of society—those in academia, religion, media, and entertainment—praise and worship the satanic trinity of Satan, the Antichrist, and the False Prophet. (Satan is laughing).

Before I lay out what I believe to be the **_mark, name,_** and **_number_** of the beast, allow me to expose two specific strategies of our adversary. First, he targeted our precious children and young adults. Satan's deceptions and toxic ideology for America accelerated approximately fifty years ago. With strategic precision, demonic forces led the Supreme Court in June 1963 to reject God and His Word by forbidding Bible reading and prayer in public schools. What a surly, arrogant move by these justices. The results have been documented. Statistically, since 1963, America has deteriorated in multiple categories—violent crime, premarital sex, sexually transmitted diseases, divorce, and SAT scores (7).

John McTernan's pamphlet, *God's Final Warning to America*, may be out of print. One of his websites is; https://usaprophecybooks.com/about-the-author/. In addition, atheistic socialist and humanist professors were allowed to invade our colleges and seminaries. They wasted no time converting marginal Christians into socialists and humanists. The ongoing apostasy also contributed to the decline of Christianity. These are some of the reasons the youth have been corrupted and often votes with socialists and humanists.

Satan exploited the weak link in our representative form of government—the Judicial Branch. Progressive activist judges realized they could 'legislate' from the bench. These judges know they can act independently from voters. The House of Representatives and the Senate have done **_nothing_** to stop this abuse of office. Essentially, the Constitution says **_only_** what these justices say it says, regardless of the plain text of our Constitution. Precedent, our Founding Fathers, and the will of the people are **IGNORED!** Brethren, this is no longer America. It is a country ran by elite judges! State's rights are a joke. This dynamic was examined in my first book; *MR PRESIDENT, I RESPECTFULLY DISAGREE,* pages 28—32.

On June 26, 2015, the Supreme Court ruled that the states cannot ban same-sex marriage. Yet even a regular citizen such as me knows that the Tenth Amendment to the US Constitution says, "The powers not delegated to the United States by the Constitution, nor prohibited by it to the States, are reserved to the States respectively, or to the people." The ruling on same-sex marriage essentially authorizes the courts to legislate morality (8). Also, this ruling essentially ignores our constitutional freedom of religion (9). In my humble opinion, the Christian cleansing of America is gaining speed every day, and, Satan is laughing.

The second beast in Revelation 13 coming up out of the **earth** is the False Prophet. He will be cheered on as he directs the masses to "make an image to the beast who was wounded by the sword and lived" (Revelation 13:14). I believe this 'image' will be a great robot-like statue that could be six-feet by sixty-six feet, or larger. It will have the facial features of the Antichrist. It will be electrified, computerized, and animated with speakers, cameras, microphones and movement gears. It will have the latest smart speaker technology. It will be able to interact verbally via 'artificial intelligence'. It will be programed to speak in any language and will possess amazing humanlike features. It can solve any problem, and answer any question. The robot will look very intimidating and powerful; it will have a deep, authoritarian voice. Anyone who refuses to respect and worship this robot image will be ___summarily executed!___

Most people alive at this time couldn't care less about the Ten Commandments. Of course, the Second Commandment says, "You shall not make for yourself any carved image, or any likeness of anything that is in heaven above, or that is in the earth beneath, or that is in the water under the earth; you shall not bow down to them nor serve them" (Exodus 20:4–5).

Possibly, a human sized Robot Idol-Image will stand in the rebuilt Jewish Temple in Jerusalem. Another larger Robot Idol-Image may be built in Vatican City, near St. Peter's Basilica in the city of Rome Italy. Rome is the Antichrist's headquarter city. A much smaller replica of the Robot Idol-Image could be required in every home, office, and place of business in the world; these Robot Idol-Images could be electrified, three-dimensional holograms or a similar image. This image will hear, see, speak, and interact with anyone nearby. Modern technology, computer animation, artificial intelligence, voice recognition, and facial recognition seamlessly integrates with the ___mark, name, and number___ technology of the Antichrist. According to Wikipedia,

"A smart speaker is a type of wireless speaker and voice command device with an integrated virtual assistant that offers interactive actions and hands-free activation with the help of one "hot word" (or several "hot words"). Some smart speakers can also act as a smart device that utilizes Wi-Fi, Bluetooth and other wireless protocol standards to extend usage beyond audio playback, such as to control home automation devices ... Some smart speakers also include a screen to show the user a visual response." (https://en.wikipedia.org/wiki/Smart_speaker)

Let us examine the mandatory policies of the second beast that comes out of the earth. The second beast is known by most Bible scholars as the False Religious System (FRS), headed by the False Prophet. The False Prophet requires every man, woman, and child to take the _mark,_ which I believe is a computer chip implant (CCI) that contains demographic, economic, medical information, and whatever else the Antichrist wants. The _number_ of the beast in my opinion is three— six-digit numbers— stacked on top of each other. Finally, the _name_ of the beast in my opinion is the official symbol of the beast kingdom. Historical examples would be the swastika (Nazis), and national flags, such as for the United States, Great Britain, and any other country. Current technologies can track internet speech, movement (GPS), cell phone activity, and essentially all human activity. Welcome to a socialist 'paradise', headed by the control freak from hell.

As always, inventions and gadgets such as guns, TV, and the internet, are neither good nor bad. The user (Humanity) determines if the use is 'good' or 'evil'. Academic constructs such as relativism, humanism, and rationalism can be, and have been abused by mankind. We need a 'user manual' for human beings. We need an authority source to determine good versus evil. God provided for these needs via the Word of God, better known as the Bible. If the source of truth is removed, chaos results. To ignore the existence of God and His declaration of truth is a fatal error. These academic doctrines and philosophies would have you believe that they are superior to holy scripture.

Bible prophesy warns that the Antichrist will use technology to intimidate, control, and dominate humanity. Satan uses as bait; 'freedom, autonomy, debauchery, and self-will'. Nothing could be further from the truth. According to current thinking, there is no truth, there is no normal; truth is what the Antichrist says is truth. Any violation of the Antichrist's socialistic bureaucracy results in a visit by the Gestapo.

Chapter 14's topics, issues, and symbols include a Lamb, Mount Zion, 144,000, seven attributes of the 144,000, Babylon falling twice, God's warning followed by His wrath, harvest time and judgment time. The Lamb of course is Jesus. Mount Zion is probably the heavenly Jerusalem or headquarters of God. The 144,000 are Jewish evangelists (Revelation 7:4–8). Babylon is the religious and political headquarters for the Antichrist's beast government and religious system. Both are probably in Rome and were described in the Prophet Daniel's interpretation of King Nebuchadnezzar's dream.

> Whereas you saw the feet and toes, partly of potter's clay and partly of iron, the kingdom shall be divided; yet the strength of the iron shall be in it, just as you saw the iron mixed with ceramic clay. "And as the toes of the feet were partly of iron and partly of clay, so the kingdom shall be partly strong and partly fragile. "As you saw iron mixed with ceramic clay, they will mingle with the seed of men; but they will not adhere to one another, just as iron does not mix with clay. (Daniel 2:41–43)

The end-time beast government will involve a unnatural coalition of ethnicities, religions, politics, and economics. Iron could represent the political/economic components, and clay could represent the ethnic/religious preferences of the revived Roman Empire.

The 144,000 had the Father's name written on their foreheads. This reinforces their identification with God the Father as He was mainly involved with the Jews. Jesus was the main person of the Godhead in the birth of the church age and the new covenant.

The Holy Spirit seems to be the main person of the Godhead during the church age. Verse 2 amplifies the powerful presence of God. Imagine you were there: "And I heard a voice from heaven, like the voice of MANY WATERS (ocean waves crashing on shore), and like the voice of LOUD THUNDER. And I heard the sounds of harpists playing their harps."

The contrast between power and gentle music reflects the multifaceted nature of our God. He can be loving, kind, and gentle, or He can be full of righteous indignation. These 144,000 Jewish evangelists have apparently completed their mission as they are pictured with Jesus on Mount Zion. I am told that time is different in heaven. God can see the past, present, and future. "But the hour is coming, and now is, when the true worshipers will worship the Father in spirit and truth" (John 4:23). Also, God is the "'Alpha and the Omega, the Beginning and the End,' says the Lord, 'who IS and who WAS and who is TO COME, the Almighty'" (Revelation 1:8). Can you see how God sees the big picture of human history?

These Jewish evangelists are totally dedicated, loyal, and obedient. They have seven traits or characteristics listed in Revelation 14:4–5. No doubt many of them have made the ultimate sacrifice—martyrdom. Their message is urgent, and it appears to be part of God's *final* appeal for salvation. Indications are that angelic beings are involved in this final invitation and appeal to humankind (Revelation 14:6, 8–9). The message from the Jewish evangelists and angels is coupled with a warning of judgment for followers of the satanic trinity. Verse 7 seems to be God's attempt to confront the current generation with the fact that the Antichrist cannot stop the four judgments on heaven, earth, the sea, and springs of water, **THEREFORE** he cannot be God! "Fear God and give glory to Him, for the hour of His judgment has come; and worship HIM WHO MADE heaven and earth, the sea and springs of water." Father God sent the same message to the Egyptians and Pharaoh, but they were stiff necked and had to learn the hard way. No doubt the generation that lives during the tribulation period will just as stubborn and arrogant. "He who is often reproved, and hardens his neck, Will suddenly be destroyed, and that without remedy" (Proverbs 29:1).

Did you catch the reference to the trinity in verses 13–14? Chapter 14 indicates that the time of harvest has come. The growth and development of the sons of God and the sons of the devil have reached their max; thus, the harvest is gathering time for good and evil.

> "Babylon is fallen, is fallen, that great CITY, because she has made all nations drink of the wine of the wrath of her fornication … If ANYONE worships the beast, and his image, and receives his MARK on his forehead or on his hand, he himself shall also drink of the wine of the wrath of God, which is poured out full strength into the cup of His INDIGNATION. And he shall be tormented with fire and brimstone in the presence of the holy angels and in the presence of the Lamb." (Revelation 14:8–10)

So much for the 'meek and mild Jesus'. He deserves total respect, reverence, and worship. If you are alive at this time, you have a big decision to make. The Antichrist claims to be god, and demands worship. The Bible, the two witnesses, the 144,000 Jewish evangelists all report that the God of the Bible is the only God. Who is your God?! Your choice could result in torture and death by the

Antichrist. On the other hand, rejecting the God of the Bible results in the wrath of God. Choosing the Antichrist buys you a few more days on earth. Choosing God could result in death by beheading, but remember, death is only a transition. Only Father God can give eternal blessings after physical death. Listen to the words of Jesus: "And do not fear those who kill the body but cannot kill the soul. But rather fear Him who is able to destroy BOTH soul and body in hell" (Matthew 10:28).

Let us return to Revelation chapter 14. Again, the phrase "is fallen, is fallen," could mean that there are two Babylon's—iron and clay, specifically, a political/economic (Iron) Babylon, and an ethnic/religious (Clay) Babylon. Both may be in Rome. The heavenly angel is announcing that God has authorized the destruction of both Babylon's. However, each will have a separate path to destruction. The word *fornication* is symbolic for illicit worship with the satanic trinity. 'Lord', 'Spirit' (v. 13), and 'Son of Man' (v. 14) refers to the true Trinity.

The end of chapter 14 and especially verses 14–20 speak of harvest time and judgment time. Six parables of Christ report in detail, important specifics about God's harvest and judgment: the ten virgins (Matthew 25:1–13), the weeds (Matthew 13:24–30), the net (Matthew 13:47–50), the watchful servants (Luke 12:35–40), the growing weed (Mark 4:26–29), and the absent householder (Mark 13:34–37). I highly recommend study of these parables.

CHAPTER 6
Revelation 15–16

Now, the final seven plagues from God. After thousands of years of long-suffering, Father God finally vents His righteous wrath "to execute judgment on all, to convict all who are ungodly among them of all their ungodly deeds which they have committed in an ungodly way, and of all the harsh things which ungodly sinners have spoken against Him" (Jude 1:15).

Some people tell me I'm attracted to bling—things that glitter and sparkle. Things like cubic zirconia, rhinestones, and sequins. Well, God's heaven and throne room are filled with awesome sights. For example, a

> "sea of glass mingled with fire, a golden crown, a rainbow was on his head, his face was like the sun, and his feet like pillars of fire, I saw seven golden lampstands, and in the midst of the seven lampstands One like the Son of Man, clothed with a garment down to the feet and girded about the chest with a golden band … His eyes like a flame of fire; His feet were like fine brass, as if refined in a furnace, and His voice as the sound of many waters; He had in His right hand seven stars, out of His mouth went a sharp two-edged sword, and

His countenance was like the sun shinning in its strength." (Revelation 15:2, 14:14, 10:1, 1:12–16)

Blingy is not the word for God's throne room; there is nothing cheap or artificial about Him. Let's look at possible meanings for these Bible descriptions and symbols. First, the sea of glass mingled with fire. Unlike our restless and dangerous oceans, glass is stable and transparent; that speaks of safety and honesty. Fire could speak of many things. According to the *Wycliffe Bible Dictionary* (page 607), fire may symbolize the divine presence, God's glory, zeal, the Holy Spirit, angels, suffering and affliction, and God's wrath. If you are reading these words during the reign of the Antichrist, notice 15:2: "And I saw something like a sea of glass mingled with fire, and those who have the victory over the beast, over his image and over his mark and over the number of his name, standing on the sea of glass, having harps of God." Did you notice four of the life-threatening issues that tribulation saints will have to overcome?

Of course Father God will be with you as you resist and defy the Antichrist. Of course that will require strong faith. All saints alive at this time will have to defy the man himself (the beast), his image-idol (False worship), participation in his government (the mark), and participation with his economic system (the number). For these saints, after severe persecution and even martyrdom, they will be welcomed into heaven as tremendous victors and overcomers. These saints sing the song of Moses and the song of the Lamb with sincerity. They have experienced firsthand His deliverance (after death) and His magnificence over evil. They remained faithful and obedient, even in the face of death. They know Him, only as martyrs could know Him.

The temple of heaven was opened, "And out of the temple came the seven angels having the seven plagues, clothed in pure bright linen, and having their chests girded with golden bands" (Revelation 15:6; see also 1:13). Brethren, can you handle a little controversy? It concerns Revelation 15:6 and 1:13. It was brought to my attention in the early seventies by an itinerant elderly saint during a home Bible study. "Pure bright linen" usually symbolizes righteousness and purity. But what does "having their chests GIRDED with golden bands" mean? This verse is translated somewhat differently from translation to translation. The KJV says, "having their breasts girded with golden girdles." Do angels need their breasts girded with girdles? Hold on; some translations read 'sashes, bands, and belts' instead of girdles. The word *sash* has multiple meanings including "an ornamental band, ribbon, or scarf worn over the shoulder or around the waist, often formally as a symbol of distinction" (*Webster's New World Dictionary*, Second College Edition). Are these angels androgynous? Or, are these golden sashes, belts, bands, or girdles symbols of distinction? We probably will not know for sure until we get to heaven.

Revelation 15:8 speaks of the immense, earthshaking power of God. Have you ever been near raw, dangerous power? How about powerful electrical facilities that are fenced, and buzz loudly so that the ground vibrates. Large conspicuous signs state; "DANGER—HIGH VOLTAGE" Another example is being dangerously close to a fast moving train that shakes the earth as it zips by. I have no doubt that the apostle John experienced the presence of God as few people have.

Let's move on to Revelation 16. Do you know people who have a startle reflex? It can range from mild to severe. In the world of audiology, it's known as acoustic shock disorder. I have a mild case of it. Especially when I'm at a movie theater and suddenly experience loud, scary scenes. My wife will tell you that my whole body jerks and clenches. Other people at the theater snicker and think it's funny. It happened one night when I was at work with children at a mental health facility. The boy next to me thought it was funny and laughed. I was not offended because I am used to that reaction. But I felt that the apostle John may have had repeated **_acoustic shock reactions_** during his great spiritual experience. No doubt John was greatly startled when he heard "A LOUD VOICE from the temple."

Before launching into the seven bowl judgments, I feel led to explain a possible rational for God's anger. A few years ago, a famous actress spoke on TV on behalf of a charity that benefits victims of various catastrophes. She seemed to blame God for allowing these catastrophes (earthquakes, floods, diseases, famines, poverty, etc.). It sounded well reasoned on the surface, but the God of the Bible does not want suffering, but healing, blessings, peace, and harmony. It is **man** who has opened the door wide for suffering. Let me explain. Blessings and curses can be found throughout the Bible. It was humankind that chose to openly sin and bring down all the curses God said would result. It started from the very beginning.

> "And the Lord God commanded the man, saying, "of every tree of the garden you may freely eat; but of the tree of the knowledge of good and evil you shall not eat, for in the day that you shall eat of it you shall surely die." When both Adam and Eve sinned, Father God said "Because you have heeded the voice of your wife, and have eaten from the tree of which I commanded you, saying, 'You shall not eat of it': CURSED is the ground for your sake." (Genesis 2:16–17, 3:17)

Later, Father God exhaustively explained the laws of blessings and curses in Deuteronomy 28. In Deuteronomy 30:19–20, He pleaded with the nation of Israel, His chosen people,

> "I call heaven and earth as witnesses today against you, that I have set before you life and death, blessing and cursing; therefore CHOOSE LIFE, that both you and your descendants may live; that

you may love the Lord your God, that you may obey His voice, and that you may cling to Him, for He is your life and the length of your days; and that you may dwell in the land which the Lord swore to your fathers, to Abraham, Isaac, and Jacob, to give them."

Do you see it? His discipline is meant to be 'therapeutic'. Choices have consequences. Reaping and sowing are among the spiritual laws that govern our existence. After thousands of years of long-suffering, sending prophets, the Messiah, and the lengthy Church Age, Father God decides to purge and eliminate the cause of suffering and curses. Brethren, even God has a limit when it comes to deliberate rebellion (Genesis 6:3). Listen—it's His cosmos, His creation. He can and will do as He sees fit. Those who choose to love and obey Him will enjoy another Garden of Eden. People who despise authority and God specifically, describe Him as a tyrant. But no tyrant would say, "As I live says the Lord God, I have no pleasure in the death of the wicked, but that the wicked **turn from his way** and live. Turn, turn from your evil ways! For why should you die, O house of Israel?" (Ezekiel 33:11). Father God's compassion is on display throughout the Bible. Two particular Old Testament scriptures reveal His compassion and mercy—2 Chronicles 36:15, 16, and Psalm 78:38, 39. Please look them up and read them.

In Romans 5:8–10, we read,

"But God demonstrates His own love toward us, in that while we were still sinners, Christ died for us. Much more then, having now been justified by His blood, we shall be saved from wrath through Him. For if, when we were enemies we were reconciled to God through the death of His Son, and much more, having been reconciled, we shall be saved by His life."

What else could he do?

All Seekers of God, Accept Christ as Your Lord and Savior

1. Admit you are a sinner.
2. Agree with God and turn (repent) from known sin.
3. By faith, believe that Jesus suffered and died to pay for your sins.
4. Prayerfully invite Jesus into your heart as your Lord and Savior.

Prayer

Dear God, I believe that your Son, Jesus, suffered and died on the cross to pay for my sins. Through faith in Christ, I accept Jesus as my Lord and Savior. Thank you for forgiving me and cleansing me from all sin. Help me to live for you and depend on you all the days of my life, amen.

The first bowl judgment (Rev chapter 16) speaks of a "foul and loathsome sore came upon the men who had the mark of the beast and those who worshiped his image." (Revelation 16:2). Brethren, if you are alive at this time, you must *not* be involved in any way with the Antichrist system. May I suggest possibilities for that "foul and loathsome sore"? Could it be a form of skin cancer, Leishmaniasis, boils, or carbuncles? Per Wikipedia,

> "Cutaneous Leishmaniasis (also known as oriental sore, tropical sore, chiclero ulcer, or Aleppo boil) is the most common form of leishmaniasis affecting humans. It is a skin infection caused by a single celled parasite that is transmitted by the bite of a phlebotomine sand-fly. There are about 20

species of Leishmania that may cause cutaneous leishmaniasis." (1)

Per the MayoClinic.org, "Boils and carbuncles are painful, pus-filled bumps that form under your skin when bacteria infect and inflame one of more of your hair follicles" (2).

If the Bible is describing a form of skin cancer, Wikipedia.org states, "There are three main types of skin cancers; basal-cell, squamous-cell and melanoma." One cause of skin cancer is ultraviolet radiation from the sun or tanning beds (3). Radiation from the sun is very relevant in that God uses the sun to "scorch men with fire" (Revelation 16:8). Satan and his followers have tried to commandeer God's earth, but Father God uses His sun and the earth to punish them. The whole world fails to understand that Antichrist is not God or else he would stop these plagues. In psychology, it's called **_delusional thinking._**

The second bowl judgment turned the sea (salt water) into blood: "and EVERY living creature in the sea died." The third bowl judgment caused the "rivers and springs of water" (fresh water) to become blood. These bowl judgments may occur in rapid succession, like the punches a champion boxer pounding on his stunned opponent.

> "Then the fourth angel poured out his bowl on the SUN, and power was given to him to SCORCH men with fire. And men were scorched with great heat, and they blasphemed the name of God who has power over these plagues; and they did not repent and give Him glory." (Revelation 16:8–9)

You talk about rebellious! I have heard of jail inmates who persist in violent resistance and end up shackled in a restraint chair with a spit bag attached to their heads. They can still curse, but nobody cares. In mental health facilities where I worked for decades, they are placed in a locked and padded room. If they were 'self-injurious' they were forcibly placed in four-point restraints to a bed. Some continue cursing, but, usually after an hour or two, they express interest in being more civil. Brute force is the only thing some people respect.

Next, the fifth angel poured out his bowl on the throne of the beast, and his kingdom became full of darkness, "and they gnawed their tongues because of the pain" (Revelation 16:10). On top of painful sores, the stench of dead oceans and rivers, add darkness. These judgments are like torpedoes from God aimed directly at the throne of the beast. But how can darkness result in pain? I believe the combination of all these plagues resulted in mental and emotional pain. As a retired mental health professional, I know that mental and emotional pain is just as miserable as physical pain. Depression and anxiety are often described as darkness, or a dark cloud. Demons of hopelessness and pessimism pile on. Thoughts of suicide can begin. Those of us who have struggled with severe depression know what I am talking about. Thank God, there are secular and biblical strategies that often help to bring relief. I learned to resist depression and discouragement by standing on the promises of God. In spiritual warfare, I have made good use of the shield of faith and the sword of the Word. I learned to quote such scriptures as "submit to God ... Resist the devil and HE WILL FLEE FROM YOU" (James 4:7). Godly counselors are very helpful. It often took perseverance, but victory was always obtained. We are not helpless victims. We need to be proactive and resist sickness, depression, or whatever the need is.

Find the relevant scriptures and confess them out loud. Finally, know that "all things work together for good to those who love God, to those who are the called according to His purpose" (Romans 8:28; 2 Peter 1:4; Ephesians 6:16–17; Romans 10:8–10). Also, success often involves guidance and support from godly counselors (Proverbs 11:14).

"Then the sixth angel poured out his bowl on the great River

Euphrates, and its water was dried up, so that the way of the kings from the east might be prepared" (Revelation 16:12). Context indicates the following. These oriental kingdoms might include; China, Japan, Korea, Vietnam, Thailand, Cambodia, and others. If you include Asia, these kings from the East might include India, Pakistan, Indonesia, Philippines, and others. These kings may be challenging the Antichrist for world domination. To convince these Eastern kingdoms to join the Antichrist's confederacy, the satanic trinity (Revelation 16:13) dispatches mighty unclean spirits. These unclean spirits (demons), perform "signs" and probably 'LYING wonders.'

> And I saw three unclean spirits like frogs coming out of the mouth of the dragon, out of the mouth of the beast, and out of the mouth of the false prophet. For they are spirits of demons, performing signs, which go out to the kings of the earth and of the whole world, to gather them to the battle of that great day of God Almighty. (Revelation 16:13–14; see also 2 Thessalonians 2:9; Deuteronomy 13:1–5)

Notice Christ intervening here saying, "Behold I am coming as a thief. Blessed is he who watches, and keeps his garments, lest he walk naked and they see his shame." Rev 16:15. Christ Himself encourages believers to hang in there and persevere! In the face of strong deception and certain martyrdom, all true believers are under incredible pressure. Brethren, all this can be avoided prior to the Rapture by sincerely repenting and accepting Christ as Lord and Savior.

The next bowl judgment seems to lead to events that culminate in global convulsions. Radical geographic and climatological events occur. If the dinosaurs could speak, they would reveal their traumatic last hours on earth. Other scriptures describe these days.

For the windows from on high are open, And the FOUNDATIONS of the earth are shaken. The earth is violently broken, the earth is split open, the earth is SHAKEN EXCEEDINGLY. The earth shall reel to and fro like a drunkard, and shall totter like a hut; its transgression shall be heavy upon it, And it will fall and not rise again. It shall come to pass IN THAT DAY that the Lord will punish on high the host of EXALTED ONES, And on the earth the kings of the earth. They will be gathered together, as prisoners are gathered in the pit, And will be shut up in the prison; After many days (1,000 years?) they will be punished. Then the moon will be disgraced And the sun ashamed; For the Lord of hosts will reign On Mount Zion and in Jerusalem And before His elders, gloriously. (Isaiah 24:18–23)

This sounds like the earth is knocked out of its orbit. Can you imagine the results of a disturbance between the orbits of earth and the moon? Tectonic plates would shift trying to adjust to radical planetary changes. A major impact event would result in such global catastrophes. Per Wikipedia,

An impact event is a collision between astronomical objects causing measurable effects. Impact events have physical consequences and have been found to REGULARY occur in planetary systems, though the most frequent involve asteroids, comets or meteoroids and have minimal impact. When large objects impact terrestrial planets like the Earth, there can be significant physical and biospheric consequences.

It **_has happened before!_** . Again, quoting Wikipedia,

"The Chicxulub crater is an impact crater buried underneath the Yucatan Peninsula in Mexico ... It was formed by a LARGE asteroid or comet about 10 to 15 kilometers (6.2 to 9.3 miles) in diameter ... The date of the impact coincides precisely with the Cretaceous—Paleogene boundary (K—Pg boundary), slightly less than 66 million years ago, and a widely accepted theory is that worldwide climate disruption from the event was the cause of the Cretaceous—Paleogene extinction event, a mass extinction in which 75% of plant and animal species on Earth SUDDENLY became extinct, including all non-avian dinosaurs."(https://en.wikipedia.org/wiki/Chicxulub_crater) But wait! Only 24 years ago "Comet Shoemaker—Levy 9 collided with Jupiter in July 1994, providing the first direct observation of an extraterrestrial collision of Solar System Objects ... fragments of the comet "collided with Jupiter's southern hemisphere between July 16 and July 22, 1994 at a speed of approximately 60km/s (37 mi/s) (Jupiter's escape velocity) or 216,000 km/h (134,000 mph) ... The Galileo spacecraft, then on its way to a rendezvous with Jupiter ... detected a fireball that reached a peak temperature of about 24,000 k (23,700 C; 42,700 F) ... Over the next six days, 21 distinct impacts were observed, with the largest coming on July 18 at 07:33 UTC when fragment G struck Jupiter. This impact created a giant dark spot over 12,000 km (7,500 mi) across, and was estimated to have released an energy equivalent to 6,000,000 megatons of TNT (600 times the world's nuclear

arsenal). https://en.wikipedia.org/wiki/Comet_
Shoemaker%E2%80%93Levy_9

Brethren, I believe Father God deliberately wanted humankind to see and record this tremendous event. It was no coincidence that the American spacecraft *Galileo* was present to record this comet impact with Jupiter. He wants us to realize how fragile and vulnerable we are. Many take it for granted that He has protected us many times since Adam and Eve.

In Revelation 16, the seventh bowl judgment brings global catastrophes that are off the scale. The seventh angel poured out his bowl into the air, which could refer to heavenly or astronomical disturbances. Of course, a major impact event would result in tremendous geological and climate changes not seen since the extinction of the dinosaurs. Verse 17 states that a loud voice came out of the temple of heaven from the throne saying, "IT IS DONE!" Could this be the voice of God? No doubt John was shaking, and so am I. This appears to be the finale. However, there are still important issues to be settled.

> "And there were NOISES, AND THUNDERINGS AND LIGHTNINGS; and there was a GREAT EARTHQUAKE, such a mighty and great earthquake as had not occurred since men were on the earth. Now the great city (Babylon?) was divided into three parts, and the cities of the nation's fell. And great Babylon was remembered before God, to give her the cup of the wine of the fierceness of His WRATH. Then EVERY island fled away, and the mountains were NOT FOUND. And GREAT HAIL from heaven (air) fell upon men, every hailstone about the weight of a talent (approximately 75 lbs.). And men blasphemed God

because of the plague of the hail, since that plague was exceedingly great. (Revelation 16:17–21)

Can you see how an impact event could cause the global destruction described in the Bible? Our former home, earth, is undergoing radical disturbances. Father God is literally **SHAKING** planet earth, temporarily inhabited by rebellious usurpers. Again, Isaiah 24:18–23 reinforces Revelation 16. Thank God believers have been Raptured (rescued) and safely with God in heaven.

Another possible scenario for the global catastrophes described in Revelation 8 and 16 is a massive solar flare or ***CORONAL MASS EJECTION.*** Per an article in *Prophecy News Watch* by Brent Miller of Ingenuity Films,

> "Many are familiar with the prophetic event within Revelation that describes one third of the Earth being burnt up along with one third of the trees and grass (Revelation 8:7). John's wording is compact and precise and tells us exactly what he's seeing. Based on the wording of the text, many theologians and astrophysicists claim that what is being described COULD BE the occurrence of a coronal mass ejection (CME) from the Sun hitting the Earth! ... John described that before one third of the Earth was burnt up, "there came hail and fire"; seemingly contradicting states of matter. As the CME continues into the troposphere, it would then vaporize all planes, birds and flying insects which also complies with the next description from John that the coming of hail and fire was "mixed with blood." The CME would then continue to the surface of the Earth where John clearly described that this hail, fire and blood is then, "cast upon the earth" -burning up one third of the trees and grass!

As you can see, John's description is specific and intended to be in chronological order; describing exactly what one would expect if an unprecedented CME did indeed strike the Earth." (4)

Hail seems to be present during many types of weather catastrophes. It is relatively rare, yet I myself have seen it numerous times. I would like to focus briefly on how hail forms. Again, according to Wikipedia;

> "Hail formation requires environments of strong, upward motion of air with the parent thunderstorm (similar to tornadoes) and lowered heights of the freezing level ... Severe weather warnings are issued for hail when the stones reach a damaging size, as it can cause serious damage to human-made structures and, more commonly, farmers' crops ... Hail forms in strong thunderstorm clouds, particularly those with INTENSE UPDRAFTS ... The growth rate of hail stones is impacted by factors such as higher elevation, lower freezing zones, and wind shear ... One of the more common regions for large hail is across mountainous northern India, which reported one of the highest hail-related death tolls on record in 1888 ... stones the size of 8 centimetres (3.1 in) in diameter fall at a rate of 48 metres per second (110 mph). https://en.wikipedia. org/wiki/Hail

At this time, the earth is battered and bleeding. The earth is grossly disfigured much as Christ's face was disfigured by sinful men.

CHAPTER 7
Revelation 17

Revelation 17's topics include the great harlot, mystery Babylon, the beast with seven heads and ten horns, many waters, the great city, and the destruction of the harlot.

Before I give my thoughts (insights Lord willing) about these verses, I will comment about the interaction between the angel and the apostle John. Remember, the apostle John was out of his element. Angels are a higher order of creation. What I am about to say is speculation. Angels may relate to humans as we relate to cats and dogs, that is, angels may not really understand our level of consciousness.

> "So he (angel) carried me away in the Spirit into the wilderness. And I saw a woman sitting on a scarlet beast which was full of names of blasphemy, having seven heads and ten horns. The woman was arrayed in purple and scarlet, and adorned with gold and precious stones and pearls, having in her hand a golden cup full of abominations and filthiness of her fornication. And on her forehead a name was written: MYSTERY BABYLON THE GREAT, THE MOTHER OF HARLOTS AND OF THE ABOMINATIONS OF THE EARTH. And I saw the woman, drunk with the blood of the saints

and with the blood of the martyrs of Jesus. And
when I saw her, I marveled with great amazement.
But the angel said to me "Why did you marvel?"
(Revelation 17:3–7)

Of course John marveled! We humans live in time and space.
The vision of Revelation was awesome, surreal, breathtaking. I
suspect angels enjoy the role of tour guide. If you look at other
close encounters between angels and humans, you will pick up
further insights about angels, for example, the interaction between
Zacharias and the angel Gabriel. In Luke 1:7, we learn that Elizabeth,
his wife, was barren, and "they were both well advanced in years."
Zacharias made the mistake of questioning the veracity of Gabriel's
message that the elderly Elizabeth would bear him a son (v. 13).
Gabriel immediately took offense and said,

> I am Gabriel who stands in the presence of God,
> and was sent to speak to you and bring these glad
> tidings. But behold, you will be mute and not able
> to speak until the day these things take place,
> because you did not believe my words which will
> be fulfilled in their own time.

Whoa ... do not mess with Gabriel!

Many other interactions between humans and angels occur
throughout the Bible. In Daniel 10, as often happened, Daniel
was wiped out and fell into a deep sleep during his supernatural
encounter. The men near Daniel at the time were not allowed to
see the vision, "but a great terror fell upon them, so that they fled to
hide themselves" (Daniel 10:7). Sometimes I fantasize about having
a supernatural encounter, but I doubt I would handle it any better
than others. You see, I am afraid of spiders, especially big spiders.

Let us try to identify the major characters in chapter 17: the
harlot (woman), many waters, and the scarlet beast. The woman

or harlot is the False Religious System (FRS). The woman also represents "that great city" (Rome). Rev 17:18. The False Prophet is in charge of the FRS. This evil harlot sits on many waters and the scarlet beast. Verse 15 defines the many waters as "peoples, multitudes, nations, and tongues." The scarlet beast is the ***political*** Antichrist. Previously, the political and religious components worked together for mutual gain. The political Antichrist knows that the religious system depends on him for its existence. Eventually, the Antichrist perceives the False Prophet and his pomp and circumstance with disdain. A harlot will do whatever is called for in exchange for money. The FRS has declared that the Antichrist is God and requires worship of the Antichrist. Listen—if you really believe that the Antichrist is God, then his ideas, ways, and means are infallible.

Father God despises the apostate religious system. His righteous description of her includes 'great harlot, fornication, drunk, abominations, and filthiness'. Verse 6 states, "And I saw the woman, drunk with the blood of the SAINTS and with the blood of the MARTYRS of Jesus." This FRS has led millions away from the true God and has killed devout Jews and Christians like a meat grinder. Now, with righteous indignation, Father God arranges the destruction of this harlot church.

In Revelation 17:8 and 17:11, the beast is the Antichrist. His political and economic system carries the FRS. The real power always resides within the political and economic foundation. The old Roman Empire and the Caesars have been dead for centuries, but just as the Prophet Daniel prophesied, both are miraculously revived for the last days. The final Antichrist and the revived Roman Empire represent Satan's best efforts. The false resurrection event greatly reinforces the delusion that the Antichrist is God. Now, Humankind is hopelessly deceived. Now, Father God decides to retake His creation. The Antichrist and the False Prophet "were cast alive into the lake of fire burning with brimstone" Rev 19:20.

Father God is not finished with Satan. He (Satan) has a different future, as described in Rev 20:1—10.

Let us examine another issue regarding the identity of the "seven kings. Five have fallen, one is, and the other has not yet come" (Revelation 17:10–11). As I understand prophesy, most of scripture is from the perspective of Israel. Hopefully, readers have their Bibles nearby as we go through these passages. World empires that would rule in the Middle East and Mediterranean region include Babylon, Medo-Persia, Greece, Rome (old Rome), and the revived Roman Empire. This is according to scripture, namely Daniel chapter 2. That adds up to five world empires. Verse 10 appears to be key. The kingdom that was ruling at the time the apostle John was alive was the first Roman Empire. The king not yet come is the final Antichrist of Revelation and his revived Roman Empire. This king "that was, (alive) and is not, (dead) is himself also the eighth, and is of the seven, and is going to perdition" (v. 11). This king is none other than the Antichrist, who was 'assassinated' and then allowed (?) to revive for a short time (Zechariah 11:17; Revelation 13:3, 12, 14). Therefore, this king is both the seventh and the eighth king of verse 11. Allow me to speculate on all eight kings of Revelation 17;

1. Nebuchadnezzar—Babylonian
2. Amel-Marduk—Babylonian
3. Cyrus—Medo-Persian
4. Darius—Medo-Persian
5. Alexander the Great—Greece
6. Emperor Domitian or Nero—old Roman Empire
7. The Antichrist (666) revived—Roman Empire
8. 'Revived' Antichrist (666)—revived Roman Empire

Notice how Old Testament prophesy dovetails with New Testament prophesy (Revelation). The ten kings of Revelation 17:12 are the same kings as mentioned in Daniel 2:44. "IN THE DAYS of

THESE kings the God of heaven will set up a kingdom which shall never be destroyed … and it shall stand forever."

I would like to elaborate on the FRS. The False Prophet is used much as Hitler used his propaganda minister Joseph Goebbels. The False Prophet controls all communications, print, broadcast, radio, and internet. The FRS repeatedly deceives the masses with propaganda and fake news. That is why God sent the 144,000, the two witnesses, and selected angels. No doubt, Satan killed as many of the 144,000 as he could get his hands on. The devil cannot stand the TRUTH. Only when allowed, was Satan permitted to kill the two witnesses, and other believers. False Christs and false prophets are steeped in LYING, ACCUSING, AND DECEIVEING (LAD). Seemingly, Satan has succeeded. Most of humanity is forced, at the point of death, to worship demons, the Antichrist, and the image of the beast. Many Bible scholars believe the FRS will be in Rome. It is no coincidence that Rome is also the headquarters of the Catholic Church. If you research its (Catholic Church) history and doctrine, you will be shocked. Possibly, the reigning Pope at the time will find common ground with the charismatic Antichrist. This evil Pope will use his influence to consolidate and unite all religions into the FRS. Of course this will require "the working of Satan, with all power, signs and lying wonders, and with all unrighteous deception among those who perish, because they did not receive the love of the truth, that they might be saved" (2 Thessalonians 2:9–10).

Now let us ponder why the political and economic component, of the Antichrist system, turns on, and destroys the religious component.. Are they not good business partners? They share a disdain for Judeo-Christian tradition. They enjoy subjugating and destroying non-believers. They have successfully consolidated and controlled the masses of humanity. They have greatly benefited from each other. It boils down to fallen and corrupted human nature. Did you notice that the 'woman' (FRS) was sitting on the beast with seven heads and ten horns? (Revelation 17:3). The FRS was sitting on the political and economic beast.

When the Antichrist no longer needs the False Prophet and his 'pomp and circumstance', his days are numbered. The real power is with the Antichrist. The False Prophet has declared Antichrist to be God. Since the masses believe it, the Antichrist can do no wrong. Both men are ambitious and treacherous. Enter the dynamic known as; 'there is no honor among thieves'. All tyrants eventually eliminate any competition, real or imagined. All tyrants manipulate others for *selfish gain*. Once power is secured, the tyrant will tolerate no competing person or department. "Power corrupts, and absolute power corrupts absolutely" (John Dalberg-Acton).

All Seekers of God, Accept Christ as Your Lord and Savior

1. Admit you are a sinner.
2. Agree with God and turn (repent) from known sin.
3. By faith, believe that Jesus suffered and died to pay for your sins.
4. Prayerfully invite Jesus into your heart as your Lord and Savior.

Prayer

Dear God, I believe that your Son, Jesus, suffered and died on the cross to pay for my sins. Through faith in Christ, I accept Jesus as my Lord and Savior. Thank you for forgiving me and cleansing me from all sin. Help me to live for you and depend on you all the days of my life, amen.

Chapter 8
Revelation 18

More spiritual fireworks are in store for John as we continue with
Revelation 18. I hope you are enjoying this as much as I am. This
book is a condensation of my more than forty years of Bible study
and research and reflects my personal pursuit of God.

Next comes the entrance of a tremendous angelic presence.

> After these things I saw another angel coming
> down from heaven, having great authority, and the
> earth was illuminated with his glory. And he cried
> mightily with a loud voice, saying, "Babylon the
> great is fallen, is fallen, and has become a habitation
> of demons, a prison for every foul spirit, and a cage
> for every unclean and hated bird!" (Revelation 18:2)

Both Babylons, the FRS, and the political and economic systems
have given themselves over to total depravity. At this time, much of
humankind has thrown off any restraint and with reckless abandon
embraced materialism and unbridled pleasures of every variety.
Godly self-control is considered foolishness.

> But know this, that in the last days perilous times
> will come: For men will be lovers of themselves,
> lovers of money, boasters, proud, blasphemers,

> disobedient to parents, unthankful, unholy,
> unloving, unforgiving, slanderers, without
> self-control, brutal, despisers of good, traitors,
> headstrong, haughty, lovers of pleasure rather
> than lovers of God, having a form of godliness
> but denying its power. And from such people turn
> away! (2 Timothy 3:1–5)

I believe the Holy Spirit has prompted me to add the following clarification about money and material goods. It is not money or material possessions that are the problem; it is the *LOVE* of them that is the problem. If we love money more than we love God, it has become our idol.

What is the passion of your life? What do you think and dream about? As always, scripture clarifies the issue.

> For the LOVE of money is a root of all kinds of evil.
> (1 Timothy 6:10)

> No one can serve two masters; for either he will
> hate the one and love the other, or else he will be
> loyal to the one and despise the other. You cannot
> serve God and Mammon (riches). (Matthew 6:24)

Father God pleads with His creation to wake up to the dangers of materialism and debauchery: "I heard another voice from heaven (God?) saying, 'Come out of her, my people, lest you share in her sins, and lest you receive of her plagues'" (v. 4). This warning to come out of any system, business, or group that is ungodly has been in holy scripture for almost 2,000 years. The choices we make define who we are.

> Enter by the narrow gate; for wide is the gate and
> broad is the way that leads to destruction, and

there are MANY who go in by it. Because narrow is
the gate and difficult is the way which leads to life,
and there are FEW who find it. (Matthew 7:13–14)

If you do not know what these verses mean, I recommend the *HCSB
Study Bible* or the *Wycliffe Bible Commentary*.

Regarding excessive worldly desires, let us consider Moses, who
displayed godly backbone in the midst of widespread evil.

By faith Moses, when he became of age, refused to
be called the son of Pharaoh's daughter, choosing
rather to suffer affliction with the people of
God than to enjoy the passing pleasures of sin,
esteeming the reproach of Christ greater riches
than the treasures in Egypt; for he looked to the
reward. By FAITH he forsook Egypt, not fearing
the wrath of the king; for he endured as seeing Him
who is invisible. (Hebrews 11:24–27)

Help us, Lord, to forsake the benefits and advantages of the
Antichrist system. Like Moses may we sacrifice any participation
in a wicked world system. May we be as fearless as Moses, who
forsook Egypt, even at the risk of his life.

Father God has caused the beast (government) with ten horns
(Ten Kings) to hate the harlot church (Revelation 17:12,16–18). The
political beast now refuses to share plunder or power with the FRS.
The political Antichrist no longer needs the FRS; he is a brutal
traitor to the core. However, the backstabbing Antichrist will be
abandoned at his time of need: "He shall come to his end, and NO
ONE WILL HELP HIM" (Daniel 11:45). Babylon is the Antichrist's
flagship city and pride and joy. The huge Robot Idol- Image made in
his likeness, stands there. All earth dwellers must bow and worship
this Robot Idol-Image, or go to the guillotine. The destruction of
the Babylon's, the FRS, and the economic hub "will come in one

day—death and mourning and famine. And she will be utterly burned with fire, for strong is the Lord who judges her" (v. 8). It is repeated twice that kings and merchants "standing at a distance for fear of her torment … will stand at a distance for fear of her torment" (Revelation 18:10, 15). I believe this could indicate nuclear destruction! An atomic bomb kills in multiple ways. Per Wikipedia and the Atomic Bomb Casualty Commission, there are "immediate and delayed atomic bomb damage in survivors … FOUR causes of injury in the bombed cities; HEAT, BLAST, PRIMARY RADIATION AND RADIOACTIVE POISONOUS GAS" (1). Everybody knows that radioactive materials can kill. Nobody wants to get close to the bomb site. Now exactly when this happens I am not sure because we know that the Antichrist is not taken prisoner until Armageddon. Obviously, his political and military status is great as he prepares for battle against God Himself (Revelation 19:19–21).

It's time for God's judgment of Satan's religious and economic system. Among Babylon's prominent sins are sorcery and murder. Add to this wholesale slaughter of devout Jews and Christians. Thank God the cosmic conflict is about to come to a righteous conclusion. Thank God, "Strong is the Lord who judges her." We were warned throughout the Bible of the consequences of worshiping false Idol-Images (see Deuteronomy 4 and especially 4:30, 31, 39, 40). Sorcery is a blatant challenge to God's authority and specifically the First Commandment. Remember, sorcery includes illicit spiritualism often with the abuse of drugs and alcohol. These particular sins are nothing new (Psalm 106:37–40; Ezekiel 20:30–31, 38; Revelation 9:20–21). They are simply repackaged by Satan for the end-time generation.

The first verse of chapter 18 implies a system of rank and hierarchy among angels. Any study of angels should include a good Bible dictionary and selected books and publications. Rose Publishing has a good pamphlet on angels: "10 Questions and Answers on ANGELS." The danger is becoming preoccupied with these spiritual creatures. Our relationship is to be with the Father, Son, and Holy Spirit. We should never seek contact with angels.

The angel Gabriel appears to be a diplomatic messenger while the archangel Michael seems connected to the nation of Israel and with protection and spiritual warfare duties. As you may recall, Gabriel was often sent to announce and proclaim. Gabriel was sent to the prophet Daniel, to the father of John the Baptist, and Mary, the mother of Jesus (Daniel 9:21; Luke 1:19, 26–38). Michael is described as "one of the chief princes" and was sent to the earth to clear out satanic resistance hindering the angel (Gabriel?) from reaching the prophet Daniel. A satanic angel prince "of the kingdom of PERSIA withstood me (Gabriel?) twenty-one days." Remember, Satan is the god of this world (2 Corinthians 4:4 KJV) and "the prince of the power of the air, the spirit who now works in the sons of disobedience" (Ephesians 2:2). This satanic angel "of the kingdom of Persia (Iran)" refused to allow Gabriel(?) to reach his assigned destination, the prophet Daniel. The archangel Michael was dispatched and let loose with some star-wars salvoes. Mr. Demonic Prince quickly retreated, and Gabriel completed his assignment with Daniel. If demonic forces will interfere with the prayers of the prophet Daniel, they will interfere with our prayers. This explains why there is often a delay in victorious answers to our prayers. We are encouraged to 'wait' on the Lord, many times in holy scripture. (Ps 27:14, Ps 37:34, Ps 33:20) Also, it looks like the angels Michael and Gabriel had to fight their way out of Persia and Greece after their assignment was complete (Daniel 10:11–21).

It appears to me that God's laws (Physical and Spiritual) are programmed, into the universe. There are physical laws and there are spiritual laws. Our choices have consequences. No one can avoid the laws of sowing and reaping. Godly choices result in blessings while ungodly choices result in curses. Deliberate sin opens the door for demons to come and live with you. Demons bring restrictions, limitations, fears, and torments. Demons are like vermin—vile, loathsome, unclean, unsanitary, filthy. They promote hatred, jealousy, fear, envy, strife, and turmoil of every kind. If you are entangled with demons, you should seek godly remedies. Consult your pastor or Christian counselor.

Are you like me? I have learned and re-learned that sin may be enjoyable, but only for a season. Consequences are inevitable and usually come sooner rather than later: "God is not mocked; for whatever a man sows, that he will also reap" (Galatians 6:7). Everything, including our own bodies, is His stuff. All creation is His stuff. Abuse of others and wealth obtained in ungodly ways lead to curses. The prisons and jails are full of such people. Every generation thinks it can cheat the system. But history repeats, as we learn the very same lessons. The parade of tyrants and benefactors, saints and sinners continues.

To be a Christian or Jew when the Antichrist is actually reigning, will of course be a time of severe persecution and death. Peer pressure will be strong. Ridicule and contempt for traditional faith will be pandemic. Dear reader, it will be much better for you to accept Christ now. After the implementation of the new monetary system (mark, name, and number), you will not be able to buy or sell anything, and that will effectively flush out all nonbelievers in Antichrist. On the other hand, to take the mark, name, and number of the Antichrist results in the wrath of God (Revelation 14:9–11).

Why not start your new life with Christ now? You will find that He is a loving, forgiving, and protective Father. In the epilogue of my first book, I quoted Hebrews 12:5–9, which describes some of His parenting skills. Life would be so much better if we consulted, and trusted in scripture. It is truly the owner's manual for humankind. In addition to God's Word, Spiritual growth is enhanced by godly pastors and counselors (Proverbs 11:14).

It seems to me that life is a test. Our words and deeds will be evaluated (Matthew 12:36–37). Yes, dear reader, our words, deeds, and choices determine our eternal destiny. We all have to navigate "the world, the flesh, and the devil" (1 Jn 2:17, 1 Jn 2:16, 2 Cor 4:4) Whom will you believe? Whom will you obey? Life is full of pitfalls, trials, and temptations. God allows testing, but if you seek His counsel, "all things are possible to him who believes" (Mark 9:23). It's not easy; we all are vulnerable to demonic attacks. At times, Evil spirits try to convince me to just 'give up', 'quit fighting it', 'go for the gusto'. We are in a lifelong struggle with sin and temptation. Thank God He does not require perfection. "If we confess our sins, He is faithful and just to forgive us our sins and to cleanse us from all unrighteousness" (1 John 1:9).

It bears repeating: "The fear of the Lord is the BEGINNING of knowledge, but fools despise wisdom and instruction" (Proverbs 1:7). If you want to know the biblical definition of "fool", it is described in detail in the book of Proverbs. I have identified many in my social circle as "fools". I try not to be judgmental or condescending. I *TRY* to "speak the truth in love" Eph 4:15 If you really learn to know God, you will learn to respect Him. "It is a fearful thing to fall into the hands of the LIVING God" (Hebrews 10:31). Yet His longsuffering and love for us is strong (Matthew 18:14; Romans 5:8; John 3:16).

Sorcery is a prominent sin of the end times (Revelation 9:21, 18:23, 21:8). Let us revisit the meaning of the word *sorcery*.

> "A sorcerer is one who is said to have superhuman or occult power by virtue of spells, magic, or secret (MYSTERY) knowledge obtained from evil spirits ... The practice of sorcery was WIDESPREAD in the surrounding ancient cultures, but Israel was prohibited from allowing sorcerers, spiritists, mediums, or such like in their midst (Ex 22:18, Lev 19:26,31, 20:27, Deut 18:10–14). It was a crime punishable by death (Ex 22:18); true also under the Middle Assyrian law code for makers of magical preparations (ANET, 184b). The reason God condemned all such practices is that magic and sorcery stem from Satanic sources.

The believer's life is to be centered in a personal relationship with the ONE, TRUE LIVING GOD. He walks humbly and trustingly with his Lord, and looks ONLY to Him in prayer for the supply of his needs."(*Wycliffe Bible Dictionary*, page 1613).

Brethren, God says what He means, and means what He says.

Chapter 9
Revelation 19–20

Revelation 19

Topics and issues for Revelation 19 include celebration for the judgment of the great harlot (FRS); Praise for 'His servants and those who fear Him'; a marriage announcement; the wife of the Lamb; inadvertent worship; the identity of the rider of the white horse (chapter 19); the robe dipped in blood; heaven's armies; the rod of iron; and the lake of fire, (Gehenna).

Could "His servants _and_ those who fear Him" (v. 5) indicate different ranks of believers? The Lamb of course is Jesus. The wife is the faithful believers, the New Testament Church of Christ Jesus. The rider of the white horse (chapter 19) is Jesus. The robe dipped in blood symbolizes the sacrifice of Christ via the crucifixion.

Revelation 19:1 says, "After these things," after the judgment of the great harlot. It is clear from scripture that Father God especially detests this worldwide FRS. Scripture uses phrases such as "Mother of Harlots" and "Abominations of the earth." This apostate FRS has corrupted and demonized humankind. Like a faithful and loving husband, Father God feels deeply betrayed by followers of this FRS. Satan has finally achieved his goal of deceiving and manipulating humankind to worship his counterfeit satanic trinity. The lessons of history and the Bible are totally ignored—original sin, Cain and

Abel, the Tower of Babel, the flood of Noah, Sodom and Gomorrah, and Christ's incarnation, crucifixion, and resurrection.

This time, the cycle of sin has gone off the charts. Mockers and scorners of the Bible abound. Debauchery is pursued with reckless abandon. Reprobates revel in their reprobation. Pride and arrogance are the norm. I have witnessed America go from a Christian nation to a nation that embraces mass murder of innocent babies, gay rights, secular humanism, socialism, so-called scientific errors of the Bible, preference for random evolution versus creationism, persecution of believers, and efforts to remove any vestige of Judeo-Christian belief (Christian cleansing). Some, but not all, American youth are influenced by ungodly parents and often atheistic, socialist college professors. The general mood or atmosphere is hostile towards traditional values. Americans and the entire world have chosen to go 'for the gusto'. The social consequences are manifold. Many churches close, or cling to life. Family-friendly TV and radio shows are rare.

> "Can you believe that our country was AGHAST at the movie industry for using the word "damn"! This occurred in 1939 in the movie GONE WITH THE WIND, with Clark Gable. Only 78 years ago! ... We have "come a long way baby." (1)

Today, cable and satellite networks routinely offer R-rated, pay-per-view, and adult, on-demand. I am told that porn is a billion-dollar business. It is so easy to access in the privacy the home. I have seen alarming estimates that even Christian men and women become entangled in internet porn. When I was in middle school, it was a scandal for a girl to get pregnant outside marriage. Now, middle schoolers know more about sex than I ever imagined. Now, preoccupation with sex and pornography has resulted in sexual disorders, crimes and diseases that are off the scale. Violent crime is pandemic. It's not random acts of violence; it's demonic acts of violence.

In my opinion, this sordid state of America and the world is due in large part to the rejection of Judeo-Christian values and especially the sin of shedding innocent blood—***abortion***. Remember what God said to Cain: "The voice of your brother's blood cries out to Me from the ground. So now you are cursed from the earth" (Genesis 4:9–11). Multiply the curse of abortion millions of times.

The spiritual laws of God are unchanging and inevitable. Yet speaking against the avalanche of popular anti-Christian TV, radio, and internet sites brings instant ridicule and scorn. Money talks, not morality. Academia, the mainstream news media, and entertainment elites revel in opposition to traditional values. The result is sin approaching the level of Noah's day and Sodom and Gomorrah. God's people are ridiculed, scorned, and, in some countries, slaughtered. Once again, it makes perfect sense for Father God to be proactive, and remove his family.

This final generation is becoming unresponsive to godly remedies. Jails and prisons are running over. Social service agencies are inundated with dysfunctional families. Public drug and alcohol facilities are overrun with applicants desperate for help. Hundreds are turned away and placed on long waiting lists. Homelessness abounds. Those who are strong physically, socially, legally, or financially, take advantage of the weak. For some, oppression is a badge of honor. "Might makes right!" Court rulings are skewed in favor of the rich and powerful. This is the 'fruit' of pagan 'values'. Con artists and scammers prey on the elderly and gullible. "If the foundations are destroyed, What can the righteous do?" (Psalm 11:3).

America, you have lost your way. History shows that radicals—progressives and socialists—promise utopia but yield only dystopia. Senator Rand Paul has a new book out exposing the dangers of socialism. The title is; ***THE CASE AGAINST SOCIALISM.*** Perhaps Romans 11 is relevant? "God has given them a spirit of stupor,

Eyes that they should not see And ears that they should not hear, To this very day." Humankind without the owner's manual, the Bible, results in chaos and disorder. Soon, the service on our national debt will lead to another financial collapse. America is severely conflicted and dysfunctional. Our disordered and divided government is unable to govern, and Satan is laughing. America now looks to secular (pagan) humanism and socialism to solve our social problems. Scripture is clear about how any society is to be built. "Woe to him who builds his house by unrighteousness And his chambers by injustice" (Jeremiah 22:13). This is reinforced by the parable of the wise and foolish builders in Matthew 7:24–27 and Luke 6:47–49. Our legislators spend billions on treatment and education, and the result is educated, drugged-up barbarians who insist on 'finding themselves'. The root of the problem is spiritual, and the remedy is the laws of God. Love is the only glue that can hold families and nations together. According to the Bible, "God is love" (1 John 4:16).

But what *IS* important to this sin-sick generation? Abortion on demand any time and any place. Access to drugs and alcohol, legalization of illicit drugs, reduction of prison sentences, replacement of traditional values with politically correct values, the veneration of nature and environmentalism, uncensored TV, radio, internet, unbalanced preoccupation with sports, recreation, and pleasures of any variety. Frauds of all kinds abound; Insurance fraud, Welfare fraud and disability fraud, Medicare fraud. Activist judges ignore the plain text of our Constitution. Political elites are given favorable treatment. However, the common man/woman are oppressed.

President Trump gave his State of the Union address most recently on February 5, 2019. Democrats were conspicuous in their negative body language when the issue of late-term abortion was mentioned. There is a controversy right now about late-term abortion and even killing babies after birth if the birth mothers want that done. The governor of Virginia sparked this controversy, and he is reportedly a medical doctor. Americans are finally seeing what abortion really is—millions of babies are medically dismembered and suctioned out of the safety of the mother's womb. A former abortion worker explained why she left the abortion industry. When a sonogram graphically showed a baby trying to avoid a doctor's death instruments, the abortion worker could no longer participate in infanticide. This former abortion worker is now a powerful adversary of the lucrative abortion industry.

Abortion is not reproductive health. Abortion is not purely a woman's right to choose. As Dr. D. James Kennedy once said, "Abortion workers had better thank God that THEIR mother was NOT pro-choice." Future generations are God's business, not solely a mother's business. Jesus set the record straight regarding feminism and feminist advocacy.

> And it happened, as He spoke these things, that a certain woman from the crowd raised her voice and said to Him, "Blessed is the womb that bore You, and the breasts which nursed You!" But He said, "More than that, blessed are those who hear the word of God and keep it!" (Luke 11:27–28)

The Word of God should be our guide. Psalm 106:37–40 directly addresses the great sin of abortion. Of course, abortion for casual and convenient reasons is tantamount to murder, a violation of the Sixth Commandment. However, it is not the unpardonable sin. Often ignored in the abortion debate is the life of the baby. As Ronald Reagan once asked, "What about the rights of the baby?"

Allow me to continue my diatribe. Is it wrong to lament the decline and fall of Christian America? It seems to me a certain percentage of new parents are headed by immature, often impudent, rash, and shameless teenage girls. Some have foul mouths, grunge and gothic clothes, facial piercings, and hair colors nature never intended. The phrase "my baby's daddy" has replaced "my husband." Some of these young girls have partners who are 'deadbeat dads'. Common sense says that these pagan parents will raise pagan children. The prognosis appears predictable unless true repentance and salvation enter the picture. Thank God for concerned relatives and Christian social workers who are called to counsel wayward youth. Those who are seek help receive Godly assistance and work their way out of negative lifestyles. As a relative of mine said, "'To err is human; to forgive is divine" (Alexander Pope, Brainy Quote.com).

All of us have made mistakes; the question is how we will deal with it. To choose the ***goth subculture*** is spiritual suicide, in my opinion (2). God forbid, but I fear many of these young parents are more interested in rock concerts, cigarettes, marijuana, booze, and the latest tech toys than in caring for and mentoring their children. Vaping, electronic cigarettes, is the latest craze. At times, weary grandparents have to step in for their impaired children who are unable to raise their own children. Some are in drug rehab. Some are in jail or legally prohibited from parenting their own children. Worldly, streetwise youth and runaways are low-hanging fruit for Satan. Again, Christian values are ridiculed. Seminary students and missionaries are considered wasted lives. Academic achievement, delayed gratification, and Judeo-Christian self-control are exchanged for rock music, superhero movies, substance abuse, sexual exploits, and the latest video games. Thank God only a minority of youth make a career in such poor choices.

The other end of the spectrum is commonsense morality, academic success, and hard work. The earned benefits of such good choices are; mental health, financial stability, and respect from family and friends. There is nothing wrong with success and material possessions; again, it is the ***love*** of money that is the problem. I have had to redirect my priorities many times. I have found that I cannot pursue God and money. It is wrong to seek status symbols and flaunt wealth. Most people are put off by self-centered, proud individuals who boast about their success, wealth, or social status. Again, scripture should be our guide.

> "Then He spoke a parable to them, saying: "The ground of a certain rich man yielded plentifully. "And he thought within himself, saying, 'What shall I do, since I have no room to store my crops?' "So he said, 'I will do this: I will pull down my barns and build greater, and there I will store all my crops and my goods. 'And I will say to my soul, "Soul, you have many goods laid up for many years; take your ease; eat, drink, and be merry." "But God said to him, 'You fool! This night your soul will be required of you; then whose will those things be which you have provided?' "So is he who lays up treasure for himself, and is not rich toward God." (Luke 12:16–21)

Let us return to our study of prophesy and specifically the book of Revelation. Please read Revelation 19:1–5. Here, we see that Father God has arranged circumstances that result in the utter destruction for the flagship city (Rome) of the Antichrist. In addition to the Antichrist's economic headquarters, the apostate church or FRS is there (Rome). The towering Robot Idol-Image stands there (Rome). It bears repeating that, at this time, Rome, is the financial capital of the world and the home of 'Mystery Babylon the Great' (FRS). Why Rome? The Roman Empire murdered Christ and destroyed Jerusalem in 70 AD. The revived alliance of nations is from the old Roman Empire. Also, the 'Holy' Roman Empire was the headquarters of the Roman Catholic Church. Also, 1 Peter 5:13 seems to be a cryptic reference to Rome.

Now, the question arises as to WHY some of the ruling elite turns on the city of Rome. Like any family or kingdom, internal jealousy and infighting develops. Rev 17:16. The 'Ten Horns' (Ten

Kings) Rev 17:12,13 are sick and tired of Rome getting the lion share of the glory and treasure. These ten kings secretly maneuver with a reluctant Antichrist to betray Rome and divide up the spoils more evenly. The Antichrist may be forced to do this in order to keep the majority of his kingdom happy. Actually, God is orchestrating all of this; Rev 17:10,12,14,16,17. Father God will always have His way. Rev 18:20, Rev 19:1—6.

Many Bible scholars consider Catholic doctrine heresy. Is it true that the Catholic Church considers Catholic Doctrine equal to Scripture? Catholic theology includes the belief that the pope is the successor to Saint Peter, that he is infallible, that he is the vicar of Jesus Christ, and that Mary is to be venerated. Could the Catholic Church transform, or metamorphose into the FRS? Only God knows for sure. In any event, only God is worthy of praise and worship. No church denomination should ever claim exclusivity or infallibility.

Revelation 19:5 encourages two groups to praise Him—those who serve Him and those who fear Him. Some people have an issue with the phrase *fear Him*. There is a big difference between anxious fear and holy fear. Anxious fear stems from threats to safety such as predators, criminals, car accidents, diseases, and so on. Holy fear is a deep reverence and respect for our Creator. I have observed that deep reverence frequently leads to genuine worship and tears of joy. These tears are often accompanied with feelings of being overwhelmed by love. Sometimes, as I sing in the choir, I feel His presence, lift my hands, and praise my Lord. I have learned to overcome thoughts of restraint and fear of being labeled a fanatic. I am no longer ashamed of my God. But as always, some people take worship to the extreme. Scripture gives guidelines for proper worship (John 4:23–24; 1 Corinthians 14). There needs to be balance and proper decorum. Worship should be carried out "decently and in order" (1 Corinthians 14:40). It annoys most people when certain church members get in the 'flesh' and scream and holler with excessive emotion. If the worship is of God, there will not be attention—seeking, chaos and disorder.

Another pitfall of some churches is pride. Some church members seem to have a superior attitude toward others. Emphasis on social and economic status is offensive to most people. Pride is a hindrance to evangelization, spiritual growth, and worship. Scripture says that "no flesh should glory in His presence" (1 Corinthians 1:29). It's not who you are; it's whose you are. If it's of God, the genuine 'fruit of the Spirit' will be in evidence. Gal 5:22—24.

In Revelation 19, a marriage announcement is made and a description of the wife is given. I believe it was Saturday, May 19, 2018, that Prince Harry married Megan Markle. I watched it on TV. What an affair! It was a royal wedding for which no expense was spared. Horse-drawn carriages, stretch limos, famous musicians, adoring crowds, designer clothing, impressive jewelry, celebrities everywhere, and a magnificent cathedral. That is probably the best man can do. But just think about what Father God has planned for the marriage of His Son! Verses 7–9 indicates it's ***our turn*** to party hearty. Do you know who the wife is? The following is a quote from the *Wycliffe Bible Commentary*, page 1518.

> "Finally, John hears voices, which he does not specifically identify (v. 6), singing the last of the songs, beginning with Hallelujah, this time, NOT because of the judgment on Babylon, but because the marriage of the Lamb is come, and His wife hath made herself ready (vv. 6–8). With this, John is commanded to write the last of the beatitudes of this book, in which it is announced that the marriage supper of the Lamb has come (v. 7). The relationship of God and Christ to the redeemed, as expressed by the terms of MARRIAGE, is frequently found in both Testaments (Hos 2:19–21 ; Ezk 16:1ff; Ps 45; Mk 2:19; 1 Cor 6:15–17; Eph

5:25–27). The bridal attire is noticeably different from the attire of the great harlot, for the holy bride wears only glistening white and pure linen (Revelation 19:8), symbol of the righteous acts of the saints. All that the NT speaks of as relating to Christ the bridegroom and the Church the bride, is now consummated."

I have heard it said that the nation of Israel is symbolically the bride of the Father and that the church is symbolically the bride of Christ.

In 19:10, John "fell at his feet to worship him. But he said to me 'See that you do not do that! I am your fellow servant, and of your brethren who have the testimony of Jesus. Worship God! For the testimony of Jesus is the Spirit of Prophesy.'" This scripture seems to indicate that the person speaking to John may have been a former resident of earth. This person or angel instantly cautioned John not to worship him but to worship only God.

Next we see the entrance of a rider on a white horse. The first time a rider on a white horse was mentioned was in Revelation 6:2. At first, I thought it was Christ. Context and the other three horsemen indicate the rider is the Antichrist. However, this time, it is the real deal. In Revelation 19:11–16, it is Jesus in His role as judge and military leader who will rule with a rod of iron. So much for the meek and mild Jesus. "He Himself treads the winepress of the fierceness and WRATH of Almighty God. And He has on His Robe and on His thigh a name written: King of Kings and Lord of Lords" (Revelation 19:15–16).

We serve a robust, assertive God who is firm but fair. He has the full range of emotions yet is perfectly balanced. He is bold but not oppressive. His words and deeds are precisely measured. His strategies transcend human comprehension. His ways are higher than ours, beyond human comprehension. He can be delicate, or massive. He most certainly can be patient and long-suffering. Yet,

"Do not be deceived, God is not mocked; for whatever a man sows, that he will also reap" (Galatians 6:7).

Dozens of prophetic signs indicate that Christ's second coming is "near, at the very doors" (Matthew 24:32–34). Rose Publishing has a pamphlet titled "100 Prophecies Fulfilled By Jesus." If the *first-coming signs* were accurately fulfilled, you can rely on the signs of the second coming to be just as accurate. Dr. Noah Hutchings, the late, great author of over a hundred books and booklets, wrote *40 Irrefutable Signs of the Last Generation*. Is anybody paying attention? Jesus told us to be ready and alert to the signs of His second coming, and these signs are now *shouting* for all to see. Matthew 24 gives at least sixteen signs of the second coming. The Old Testament prophets, and especially Daniel, give many more. Like birth pangs, these signs can no longer be denied or brushed off. Strong, undeniable labor pains are occurring. Ready or not, He is coming!

In 2 Timothy 3:1–5, we can read about approximately twenty-one signs, and the increase in narcissism and pride. Pride has become prevalent in our country; that is another sign of the soon coming of Christ. "But know this, that in the LAST DAYS perilous times will come: For men will be lovers of themselves, lovers of money, boasters, PROUD" (2 Timothy 3:1–2). Of course, PRIDE is the signature sin of Satan.

Think of a Volkswagen Beetle lining up to race in the Daytona 500, or a mule lining up to race in the Kentucky Derby, or worse, humankind gathering to fight its Creator. "And I saw the beast, the kings of the earth, and their armies, gathered together to make war against Him who sat on the horse and against His army." That's it!—closing time! The sharp sword, the Word of God, instantly accomplishes the will of the Father (Rev 19:15, 19). There is no war. Immediately, rebels are defeated, disarmed, and captured. Now the wicked angels and earth dwellers will walk into God's court room in shackles and disgrace. Utter destruction awaits those who willfully defy the living God (Revelation 21:8). "It is a fearful thing to fall into the hands of the living God" (Hebrews 10:31).

Revelation 20

Dear reader, there are three chapters left in Revelation. After the examination and discussion of Revelation, we will take a brief look at how and why sociopaths develop and even accepted. We will look (briefly) at the childhood traumas and personality development of Adolf Hitler. Without checks and balances, such as in the US Constitution, tyrants will muscle their way to power.

It is clear to me that we are approaching the Rapture of the church. The Church Age is about over. The signs and birth pangs strongly indicate the soon coming of our Lord and Savior, Jesus. In my first book, I documented the fulfillment of ten signs. There are tons of other books that document many more active and flashing signs of our _current_ generation. Those who are scripturally wise should watch any leader who suddenly achieves prominence, a leader with oratory and persuasive skills. A leader with questionable roots, and good at **_SUBTERFUGE_** . That person _could_ be the final Antichrist. Especially if he has a tendency to _lie, accuse, and deceive_ (LAD). Is he a narcissist? Is he hostile to traditional authority figures? Does he deny the historical evidence of Jesus, and absolutely deny the divinity of Christ? If so, red flags should immediately go up. Barack Obama was not a perfect match. But his words and deeds caught my attention. In my opinion, his political career scored high on 'Antichrist traits'. Remember, _liar, accuser, and deceiver_ (LAD); these are names and character traits of Satan (3). The final Antichrist, whoever he is, will excel at these abilities.

Is it true that Barack Obama was associated with the author of _Rules for Radicals_, Saul D. Alinsky? It is true that Alinsky acknowledged Lucifer in his book as "the very first radical ... who rebelled against the establishment and did it so effectively that he at least won his own kingdom—Lucifer"? Wikipedia reports regarding Alinsky,

"Shortly before his death, he had discussed life after death in *Playboy*.

ALINSKY: If there is an afterlife, and I have anything to say about it, I will unreservedly choose to go to hell.

PLAYBOY: Why?

ALINSKY: Hell would be heaven for me ... Once I get into hell, I'll start organizing the have-nots over there." (4)

Of course, Lucifer became Satan. He successfully deceived Eve. At first, she listened to Satan and began to distrust God. As she continued to listen to the devil she disobeyed God. Previously, Adam and Eve had a wonderful relationship. But, malcontents love to sow divisions and dissensions (Romans 16:17). Socialists garner instant support when they sow distrust for the 'evil' rich. But, many have worked hard, trusted God, and achieved rags-to-riches success stories. Of course, there are evil poor people, and evil rich people. I've lived paycheck to paycheck most of my life. I know what it means to stay one step ahead of losing my home or my car. I know what the Bible says about hard work versus laziness. (See the book of Proverbs) History shows that demagogues and socialists trumpet pie-in-the-sky promises that never come to pass. They love to camouflage their selfish agenda as compassionate. Socialists gain favor much as modern day 'Robin Hoods'. They often have a hidden agenda, such as getting elected. Again, the book of Proverbs has a lot to say about lazy people. Is this why certain unmotivated people are attracted to socialists, communists, and con artists of every stripe? Hitler presented himself as a savior of Germany, but once he had firm control of the nation, totalitarianism and fascism was the fruit. Listen! Jesus said "You will know them by their **FRUITS**. Matt 7:16 Will humankind ever learn?

Is it true that successful entrepreneurs from other countries often have to flee their home countries when socialists can legally redistribute (steal) their hard-earned money? These small and large business owners often take the jobs they have created to countries with less regulation and taxes. I can only touch the surface of these political strategies. Of course former President Obama was not guilty of murder and terror. But he was influenced by nonbiblical authorities such as liberal Universities, authors, Ministers, news media and his preferred social circle. Scripture says; "Knowledge puffs up, but love edifies." 1 Cor 8:1. Most Americans were pleased with Barack Obama. Yet scripture warns us, "Woe to you when all men speak well of you, For so did their fathers to the FALSE PROPHETS" (Luke 6:26). Most Americans had no idea Obama would promote anti-American, anti-Christian, socialism, essentially open borders, extreme deficit spending, the (un)sanctity of life (Abortion), the (un)biblical definition of marriage(Same-Sex Marriage), politicization of the FBI, IRS, and the DOJ, and radical environmentalism.

Extreme environmentalism is essentially worship of creation rather than the Creator. (Romans 1:25). Yes, we should be good stewards of God's earth (Rev 11:18). We should honor the Creator more than creation. I find the 'Gaia Hypothesis' interesting. The Gaia hypothesis, proposes that" living organisms interact with their inorganic surroundings on earth to form a synergistic, self-regulating, complex system that helps maintain and perpetuate the conditions for life on the planet. The hypothesis was formulated by the chemist James Lovelock and codeveloped by the microbiologist Lynn Margulis in the 1970s. Lovelock named the idea after Gaia, the primordial goddess who personified the earth in Greek mythology. In 2006, the Geological Society of London awarded Lovelock the Wollaston Medal in part for his work on the Gaia hypothesis" (5). God's ways are beyond finding out.

Obama's preference for Muslims and illegal immigrants over Christians and law-abiding citizens was another wake-up call (6). Remember "Obama's Deal: $150 Billion to Iran to Destroy Israel with Conventional Arms, by Rabbi Aryeh Spero" (7). I documented Obama's assault on Christianity in my first book. I also quoted Christ as He taught how to discern false prophets. Obama's mentors and associates included; Frank Marshall Davis, Reverend Jeremiah Wright, Bill Ayers, Eric Holder, and Van Jones. (8). His father, Barack Obama Sr., had a strong influence on the former president (9). According to one book about former president Obama, he disliked rich capitalists as oppressive and exploitive of Third World countries (10). But, surely, there had to be some benefits to development of natural resources in the developing countries of Africa, Asia, Latin America and Oceania.

What happens to individuals who feed on lies and refuse to acknowledge the truth? According to scripture, deliberate acceptance of known sin and refusal to acknowledge truth, can result in "defective reasoning" (Romans 1:21, 28–31, 11:8–10; Ephesians 4:18). Father God will allow strong delusion for such people (2 Thessalonians 2:9–12). These scriptures explain how gullible humans will be blinded (deceived) and accept another monster like Adolf Hitler. Could defective reasoning be happening **right now** to liberals and progressives?

The last presidential election indicated a return to law and order, traditional family values, compassionate capitalism, and common sense. Hopefully, common sense will continue as liberals and progressives promote bizarre sexual ideas, higher taxes, open borders, abuse of office, activist judges and other left-wing agenda's. In my opinion, liberals sugarcoat their agenda and wrap themselves in 'compassion and humanitarianism'. Their not so hidden agenda is 'socialism' and 'secular humanism'. As always, look for who support Judeo-Christian values. Those who value a strong Military, **LEGAL** immigration and protection for the Homeland. It may be to late to save the economy from reckless deficit spending. Judicial reform, with a return to the Constitution as basis for law. Limited government that serves the people, rather than government that *rules* the people.

As I have said many times, one of the prominent signs of the second coming is *deception* . It was the first sign Jesus gave in the Olivet Discourse (Matthew 24:4). Unfortunately, many American youth are attracted to specious and spurious babblings of academics and news media elites. They have not learned to think for themselves. Thank God for Americans who are clear thinking, and possess common sense. Clear-thinking Americans refuse to be led around by biased and subjective news networks. Also, I question dubious 'opinion polls'. All the polls and pollsters were *wrong* the night Donald Trump was elected. God help us when the 'moral majority' is no longer a significant influence.

Hopefully, our nation is finally waking up to the propaganda put forth by news media, college professors and entertainment elites. Regular Bible study and prayer gave me the ability to discern good from evil. There is a strong need for objective and truthful news. I firmly believe that the Bible and the Holy Spirit can enable a person to discern truth from error. The youth may have suffered from 'revisionist' history books, and teachers. Many college graduates 'contract disdain' for America. They are not excited about American history and the struggle for independence from England. They forget that many of their grandfathers fought socialists and fascists in World War II. Even the bloated and arrogant NFL is learning that Americans value patriotism. No country is perfect. Injustice will never be totally eradicated. However, if America is so bad, why do the masses seek to come here from all over the globe?

We are what we eat, and we are what we think. We have become prosperous and apathetic. Many assume God would never punish America. But the truth is we have lost our zeal for God and Country. Any dead fish can float downstream; it takes a living and determined fish to swim against the tide. May we be proactive and promote solutions, rather than complain and do nothing. Lord, help me never to be ashamed of you. "For whoever is ashamed of Me and My words, of him the Son of Man will be ashamed" (Luke 9:26).

I repeat, former President Obama did not impress me as a patriotic, law and order type of candidate. Many books have exposed his political and religious preferences. Former President Obama *did* catch my attention as a prospect for 'Antichrist'. During his presidency, he repeatedly offended many Christians, including this author. I tried to evaluate him according to scripture in my first book. His charisma and speeches caused many to go beyond approval to passionate allegiance. Some even mentioned the word *messiah* along with news reports about him (11). I believe God has led me and other prophesy enthusiasts to sound the alarm for this generation. I am convinced we are near the Rapture of the Church. Scripture indicates that a *false messiah* will appear after the Rapture (2 Thess 2:6—12, 1 Thess 1:10, 1 Thess chapters 4 and 5, especially 5:9).

Call me a bible 'nut case' if you want. I am not ashamed of being a fervent believer. Within the next few years, or decades, we will see who was sane, and clear headed. I will gladly take abuse for standing for biblical themes. Spiritual opposition has only increased my desire to complete this book. I pray this book opens many eyes. I believe the *event of the ages* is upon us!

Topics and issues in chapter 20 include the possible identity of the angel that "arrested" the dragon, the Millennium or Kingdom Age, Satan's release after a thousand years, and the great white throne judgment (according to works!). I would like to examine Biblical words related to incarceration and punishment. These include; *death, hell, hades, Sheol, Tartarus*, the *bottomless pit*, the *abyss*, the *lake of fire*, the *second death*, and *Gehenna*. Finally, make sure your name is written in the *Book of Life.*

Who else but Michael the Archangel would be given the honor of capturing, chaining, and incarcerating Satan? He appears to be the angel God chose to defend Israel (Daniel 12:1). The great angel Michael was the one God sent to contend with the devil regarding the dispute about the body of Moses (Jude 9). In Revelation 12:7, Michael was the one God sent to fight against the dragon and his angels.

After all the mayhem and rebellion in human history, why in the world would God allow Satan to be released after a thousand years? The Kingdom Age should be like the Garden of Eden. Christ and His believers will be in charge. Could it be that untested faith is unreliable? With Satan being incarcerated, the millions born during the Millennium have never been tested. Struggles over tests and temptations confirms and strengthens genuine faith. Genuine Faith, is faith in God, not faith in self. It must be learned. Even Jesus was "led up by the Spirit into the wilderness to be tempted by the devil" (Matthew 4:1). Notice that Father God allows us to be tempted and tested by Satan. Only genuine faith in God can successfully overcome the world, the flesh, and the devil. God provides the spiritual weapons, that if used, always lead to eventual victory (Ephesians 6:10–18) Of special importance is the shield of faith (Ephesians 6:16). The believer must live by faith (Romans 1:17; Galatians 3:11). Also, "without FAITH it is impossible to please Him" (Hebrews 6:6). If you are submitted to God and resist the devil, "HE WILL FLEE FROM YOU" (James 4:7). "For whatever is born of God overcomes the world. And this is the victory that has overcome the world—our FAITH. Who is he who overcomes the world, but he who BELIEVES that Jesus is the Son of God?" (1 John 5:4–5). Yes, it can be done. It may take a lifetime or even death, but scripture guarantees eventual victory.

Again, those born during the millennium have never been tested. You would think the decision to follow Christ would be a no-brainer. It is a no brainer for those of us who have had to deal with sin and Satan. But, for those born during the Kingdom Age, peace, prosperity, and harmony is all they know. People born during the millennium are like Adam and Eve. They are like innocent children who know nothing of the perils of sin. Initially, it is normal and natural for them to 'trust and obey'. But if given a choice (Satan), if tempted to choose, some will find 'fault' with God and experiment with disobedience. Eve was such a person. All of us have the potential to experiment with sin. When Eve did not immediately drop dead, Adam joined with her and the Serpent. The result was that all of us were born with Satan's sin nature. All of us have sinned and tried to go our own way, but sooner or later, we learn that God's ways are best. The smart ones learn to trust and obey. I recall the old gospel hymn "Trust and obey, for there is no other way" (lyrics by John Henry Sammis, music by Daniel Brink Towner).

Perhaps God deliberately uses Satan to draw out the ones who are proud and self-willed. I certainly had to learn the hard way that God's ways are best. As I said previously, victory over the world, the flesh, and the devil is indeed possible; I did not say it was easy. Some become weary of fighting and give up. Some settle into a pattern of defeat. (Satan is laughing) Some become bitter and blame God for all their problems.

Persistent sin attracts other demons seeking to influence and control you. Demons are quick to see weakness of any variety. Persistent sin leads to strongholds of Satan. When that happens, you need extra help to get free. Sin is as toxic to humans as kryptonite was to Superman. Call on God! Call on godly counselors who know how to do spiritual warfare! "Jesus said to him, 'If you can believe, all things are possible to him who believes'" (Mark 9:23).

Does salvation mean no more trials and tribulations? Oh no. God wants sons and daughters with backbones. He wants children willing to develop into spiritual warriors. He prefers believers who develop into overcomers. Spiritual strength and maturity takes a lifetime of training and practice. All of the great characters of the Bible were 'tried and tested'. Look at the blessings given to those who overcome in Revelation 2–3. You and I can learn to do exploits for our God. This book is a work of faith that has required me to face many battles, setbacks, and discouragements. I have had to endure physical, emotional and spiritual hardships. Some people who know me snicker at the thought that God would use me. I may be a nobody in the world's eyes, but faith, as in Mark 9:23 permits God to use anybody who trusts in Him. I give the glory to God. I know that I have little to offer God. He knows how often I have given in to defeat. He knows all about my past compromises with the forces of evil. Brethren, if He will put up with me, He will love and train any true believer. I know well the scriptures "Without ME you can do nothing" (John 15:5) and "I can do all things through Christ who strengthens me" (Philippians 4:13). Hallelujah!

How should we approach God? Psalm 100 is one of the ways; I call it singing, thanksgiving, and praise (STP). Try that during your morning devotional. Psalm 15 is another way to open doors to the presence of God. A possible acronym is; URTG: walk Uprightly, work Righteousness, speaks the Truth, and follow the Golden rule. Of course the Golden Rule states; "And just as you want men to do to you, you also do to them likewise" (Luke 6:31). Psalm 15 describes those who will be permitted access, and those who demonstrate words and deeds that are indicative of genuine godliness. Of course, the fruit of the Spirit takes a lifetime to fully develop. Salvation is for whosoever. But salvation is just the beginning. Close fellowship with God is gradually developed by those who persevere and overcome (Jeremiah 29:13; Matthew 13:11–16; Psalm 91). I am speaking to myself as well as anyone else. I would love a deeper and closer relationship with Father God. The difficulty is maintaining the desire and perseverance in the face of daily distractions, and frequent trials and tribulations.

Believe me, the trials and tribulations of life will make us bitter, or better. Also, we can bring on additional heartache by deliberately disobeying the Lord. The path to a real relationship with God is fraught with difficulties. I believe this was deliberate to filter out those who lack commitment. Regarding sin, simply repent and determine to move on with the Lord. The prophet Jonah found out the hard way that disobedience brings discipline. The demons who 'sit' on our shoulders can sound so appealing! They may say, "Just give up and give in. How much more can one man take?" Many times, I have had to stand by faith, not knowing the outcome. Throw yourself onto the mercy of God: "And the Lord, He is the One who goes before you. He WILL BE with you, He will not leave you nor forsake you; do not fear nor be dismayed" (Deuteronomy 31:8). Lord, help me to keep my eyes on You, not on adverse circumstances. The book of Job reveals how to respond when, 'Bad things happen to good people'. Sometimes, ___LIFE IS NOT FAIR!___

The cosmos, including humankind, is all His stuff. Our bodies, souls, spirits, the earth, moon, and stars—they are all His stuff (1 Chronicles 29:10–16). "We are the clay, and you our potter; And all we are the work of Your hand" (Isaiah 64:8). Yes, life can be rough even for the godly: "Many are the afflictions of the righteous, But the Lord delivers him out of them all" (Psalm 34:19). But let it become an opportunity for growth. Do not give up or become bitter. I became angry with God when my precious six-year-old son was hit by a car and almost died. I blew off the faint, 'still, small voice' that told me he would fully recover. I made the common mistake of looking at the circumstances, rather than via the eye of faith. He was in a coma. He was covered with medical wires and tubes. Medical machines were beeping and graphing his vital signs. I chose not to believe the 'still small voice'. He ___did fully recover,___ but it took almost a year for him to heal from all his injuries. I had to relearn the meaning of faith. I had to learn that our children are loaned to us and are not our possessions. Father God patiently waited for me to sort out this trauma. He desires mature, assertive children who wisely navigate the twists and turns of life.

In my youth, I had a tendency to avoid confrontation. When I was much younger, I would run and hide from threatening situations. In my 50's and 60's I have learned that 80% of the time, just showing up and facing the issue often results in success. Simple prayer and sincere trust in God (not self) is a winning formula. The Serenity Prayer comes to mind. According to Wikipedia, the

Serenity Prayer was written by American theologian Reinhold Niebuhr. The best-known version; "GOD, grant me the serenity to accept the things I cannot change, Courage to change the things I can, And wisdom to know the difference" (https://en.wikipedia.org/wiki/Serenity_Prayer).

What about you? What choices will you make in the storms of life? This is what life is all about. God will evaluate the choices we make. He wants us to trust Him and learn to overcome through faith in Him. Life is full of threatening challenges. Will we follow an invisible, often silent God by faith, or will we serve the world, the flesh, and the devil?

Most church-attending Christians have heard of the 'great white throne judgment'. Revelation 20:11–15 is where you will find it. According to the *Wycliffe Bible Dictionary* (page 977), there are "at least seven distinct Divine Judgments described in the Bible." Most of my sources agree that the white throne is the judgment of the impenitent or unrepentant dead; their bodies are dead but their spirits are very much alive. I like the *Ryrie Study Bible* comments.

> "Revelation 20:11–15 … Here is pictured the judgment of the UN-believing dead. It occurs at the close of the millennium; it is based on works, in order to show that the punishment is deserved (v. 12, though of course these UN-saved people are first of all in this judgment because they REJECTED CHRIST as savior during their lifetimes) ; and it results in everyone in this judgment being cast into the Lake of Fire. This is the resurrection unto condemnation." (John 5:29)

My pastor once said, "The more I learn about God, the more I respect and reverence Him." I agree. The daily news covers blue collar, and white collar crime. The increased frequency and intensity of crimes indicates that most people have lost their fear of God. They have no idea whom they are messing with. He could prevent their next breath should He desire.

Revelation 20:14 brings up four issues I will touch on—death, Hades, the lake of fire, and the second death. In addition we will add Tartarus, Sheol, hell, abyss, Gehenna, and the bottomless pit. Most people agree about the meaning of physical death. The soul and spirit are not physical. The 'second death' is mentioned in the *Wycliffe Bible Commentary* (page 1521).

> 'But no one will be able to escape this judgment. The dead will be called forth from their graves, and from the sea, from Hades itself (v. 13); and those whose names are not found in the Book of Life will be cast into *the Lake of Fire,* which is the second death (v. 14). The records of every human life in this vast assembly will then be produced. Death itself, it seems, is not abolished until the Great White Throne is set up, and human destiny is forever settled. If we believe and embrace with joy the promises of eternal glory that are in this book, we MUST also believe with equal conviction that this terrible doom of the UNREPENTANT dead is equally true.'

Notice the great difference for those humble and meek souls who have accepted Christ, those who live by faith in a magnificent Creator.

> 'For the BELIEVERS there remains only a judgment of valuation and rewards, since Christ has kept the law in their stead and suffered and died in their place (Isa 53:5, 10,11) under the penalty of the broken law (2 Corinthians 5:21).' (*Wycliffe Bible Dictionary*, 977)

Hades is mentioned in the *Wycliffe Bible Dictionary* (pages 740–41).

> 'Luke 16:23 (ASV, RSV). This is a clear reference. Hades is used of the place of torment as distinguished from the place of bliss ... But in any case the word is used to designate a place of punishment ... Acts 2:27,31 (ASV, RSV). This passage is complicated by the fact that it is an OT quotation and its exact meaning unsure. A common view is that this refers to Christ's descent into the realm of the dead to preach to sinners or to deliver righteous ones from the upper compartment of Hades into heaven ... Christ had already spoken of Hades as a place of torment ... Revelation 1:18; 6:8; 20:13-14 (ASV, RSV). These verses also are figurative. In the first (Revelation 1:18) Christ hold the keys of hades and death. This expression reminds one of "gates of hades" in Mt 16:18 (ASV). Hades is pictured as a walled city, in this case a prison possibly. In the next passage (Revelation 6:8) hades is also linked with death and they are personified as enemies of God and men. In Revelation 20:13–14 death and hades are linked again and they deliver up the wicked dead who are in them for final judgment. This usage is reminiscent of the passage in Luke 16:23 and strengthens the idea that in the NT, Hades signifies the abode of the wicked dead.

When I looked up the phrase *lake of fire* in the *Wycliffe Bible Dictionary*, it said "See Gehenna." So apparently they are closely related. Again according to the *Wycliffe Bible Dictionary* (pages 661–62),

'The word is used as the metaphorical name of the place of TORMENT of the wicked after the final judgment ... The idea of a place of eternal spiritual punishment by fire is frequent in the OT (cf. Deut 32:22) ... This concept, combined with Jeremiah's prophecy of evil against the valley (Jer 19:2–10) developed a belief in a place of spiritual punishment to which the dread name Gehenna was given ... Jesus spoke of Gehenna as a place of future punishment ... The NT clearly teaches that the punishment of Gehenna is eternal (Mark 9:47–48; Matthew 25:46; Revelation 14:11).'

Next is the bottomless pit. *Wycliffe* (page 270) reads,

'The expression occurs only in Revelation 9:1,2, where at the sound of the fifth angel the pit was opened by one possessing the key and beings came forth resembling locusts, but having faces like men (Revelation 9:7) ... This third realm called the ABYSS was also called HADES (Gr. In LXX of Psalm 139:8) and considered to be the abode of the dead (Romans 10:7; Acts 2:31) and of demons (Luke 8:31). The devil himself is kept in the abyss according to John's revelation (Revelation 20:3).'

So the bottomless pit and the abyss are related.

Three more related words to go—Tartarus, Sheol, and hell. I could not find Tartarus in my Bible dictionaries, but I did find it in one of my secular dictionaries. Per *Webster Illustrated Contemporary Dictionary, Encyclopedic Edition* (page 753): "The abyss below Hades where Zeus confined the Titans." I am not a believer in Greek mythology; I am simply quoting that dictionary. Apparently, Tartarus is simply another word related to Hades.

Next is Sheol. *Wycliffe Bible Dictionary* (page 1572) reads,

> 'The Hebrew word sheol is of uncertain derivation and was apparently not used in Semitic languages outside of Jewish circles. It is used in the OT 65 times, translated in the KJV 31 times by "grave," 31 times by "hell," and three times by "pit." The ASV and RSV uniformly transliterate it by "Sheol." There are difficulties with its interpretation. The best tool in its study is a concordance. The usual view is that Sheol is the place of departed spirits (BDB, ISBE, HDB, etc.). BOTH the righteous (Gen 37:35) and wicked go there (Proverbs 9:18).'

Finally, the word that everybody knows—'hell, in common and theological usage, the place of future punishment of the wicked dead. However, since the KJV uses "hell" to signify the grave and the place of disembodied spirits good and bad alike, care must be taken to prevent mistakes and confusion.'

> 'Hell, in the sense of a place of future punishment, is certainly distinctly taught in the Bible ... such words and descriptions as given are metaphors to express the TERRIBLE AGONIES of the soul as it suffers endless remorse in eternity to come, when SEPARATED from God and all that is good and CONFINED with all that are bad ... The four words translated 'hell' are; 1. Sheol. 2. Hades. 3. Gehenna. 4. Tartaroo.' (*Wycliffe Bible Dictionary* pages 778–79)

Chapter 10
Revelation 21–22

Revelation 21

Now for the good stuff. It's God's turn to 'wow' His beloved creation. We all know life's limitations and vulnerabilities. That was then; this is now. Get ready for life without the curse (Genesis 3). No more sickness, pain, stress, or death. Whether we are pre-trib, post-trib, or tribulation martyrs, we now soak in the sights and sounds of heaven. Imagine your ability to sense multiplied by 10. Heaven will exceed any 3-D effects, surround-sound speakers, wind and water effects, and programmed seat movements.

Father God has been preparing for this moment for thousands of years. Similar to a loving father who secretly and cheerfully puts out Christmas presents for his children the night before. Christmas morning dawns, and a loving mother hears her children stirring in their bedrooms. She nudges her husband to wake up. Soon, the oohs and ahhs and shouts of joy from precious children blend with the sound of wrapping paper being shredded. But this time, the God of the universe has unlimited funds to provide unlimited blessings.

Our new reality is a multidimensional world with colors never seen before—angelic beings move about, and our senses are overwhelmed. Words such as 'AWESOME' and 'WONDERFUL' apply. Feelings of LOVE and ACCEPTANACE abound. Let's take a peek at our new home.

145

'And I saw a NEW heaven and a NEW earth, for the first heaven and the first earth had passed away. Also there was NO MORE SEA. Then I, John, saw the Holy City, New Jerusalem, coming down out of heaven from God, prepared as a bride adorned for her husband. And I heard a loud voice from heaven saying, "Behold, the tabernacle of God is with men, and He will dwell with them, and they shall be His people, and God Himself will be with them and be their God. "And God will wipe away ever tear from their eyes; there shall be *no more* death, nor sorrow, nor crying; and there shall be *no more* pain, for the former things have passed away." Then He who sat on the throne said, "Behold, I make all things new." And He said to me, "Write, for these words are true and faithful." And He said to me, "It is done! I Am the Alpha and the Omega, the Beginning and the End. I will give of the fountain of the water of life freely to him who thirsts. "He who overcomes shall inherit all things, and I will be his God and he shall be My son. "But the cowardly, unbelieving, abominable, murderers, sexually immoral, sorcerers (drug-addicts), idolaters, and all liars shall have their part in the lake of fire which burns with fire and brimstone, which is the second death." Then one of the seven angels who had the seven bowls filled with the seven last plagues came to me and talked with me, saying, "Come, I will show you the bride, the Lamb's wife." And he carried me away in the Spirit to a great and high mountain, and showed me the great city, the Holy Jerusalem, descending out of heaven from God, having the glory of God. And her light was like a most precious stone, like a jasper stone, clear as crystal. Also she had a great and high wall with twelve gates, and twelve angels at the gates, and names written on them, which are the names of the twelve tribes of the children of Israel; three gates on the east, three gates on the north, three gates on the south, and three gates on the west. Now the wall of the city had twelve foundations, and on them were the names of the twelve apostles of the Lamb. And he who talked with me had a gold reed to measure the city, its gates, and its wall. And the city is laid out as a square, and its length is as great as its breadth. And he measured the city with the reed; twelve thousand furlongs. Its length, breadth, and height are equal. Then he measured its wall; one hundred and forty-four cubits, according to the measure of a man, that is, of an angel. And the construction of its wall was of jasper; and the city was pure gold, like clear glass. And the foundations of the wall of the city were adorned with all kinds of precious stones; the first foundation was jasper, the second sapphire, the third chalcedony, the fourth emerald, the fifth sardonyx, the sixth sardius, the seventh chrysolite, the eighth beryl, the ninth topaz, the tenth chrysoprase, the eleventh jacinth, and the twelfth amethyst. And the twelve gates were twelve pearls; each individual gate was of one pearl. And the street of the city was pure gold, like transparent glass. But I saw no temple in it, for the Lord God Almighty and the Lamb are its temple. And the city had no need of the sun or of the moon to shine in it, for the glory of God illuminated it, and the Lamb is its light. And the nations of those who are saved shall walk in its light, and the kings of the earth bring their glory and honor into it. Its gates shall not be shut at all by day (there shall be no night there). And they shall bring the glory and the honor of the nations into it. But there shall by no means enter it anything that defiles, or causes an abomination or a lie, but only those who are written in the Lamb's Book of Life.' (Revelation 21)

Was it jasper or diamond? This is according to Wikipedia.

"Jasper, an aggregate of microgranular quartz and/or chalcedony and other mineral phases, is an opaque, impure variety of silica, usually red, yellow, brown or green in color; and rarely blue." (https://en.wikipedia.org/wiki/Jasper)

Diamond on the other hand "is a solid form of the element carbon with its atoms arranged in a CRYSTAL structure called diamond cubic" (https://en.wikipedia.org/wiki/Diamond).

Revelation 21:11 says, "And her light was like a most precious stone, like a jasper stone, clear as crystal." A diamond would seem to best fit this description. Only Father God knows for sure. Also, chalcedony is listed as the third precious stone that adorned the foundations (Revelation 21:19).

There are other uncertainties in the Bible such as 'gopherwood' (Genesis 6:14). Was it cypress or cedar? The "two witnesses' (Rev 11:3—12). Were they Moses and Elijah?

Father God knows we like new things. Jesus delights in showing us our new living quarters.

In my Father's house are many mansions; if it were not so, I would have told you. I go to prepare a place for you. And If I go and prepare a place for you, I

will COME AGAIN and receive you to Myself; that
where I am, there you may be also. (John 14:2–3)

If you like that new-car smell, the smell of fresh paint, new-carpet
and so on, you'll be ecstatic because it is yours at no cost. Our new
earth and new heaven will be refreshingly different. There will
be no dangerous, tempestuous seas. It looks to me that all of us,
whether Jew or gentile, all who have accepted Christ, will be living
in God's house as one big happy family!

When I was first married, I suggested to my mother-in-law
that we all chip in and buy a large house and live happily ever after.
My mother-in-law had three children. She had more wisdom and
experience than I did. She said, "Joe, we'd all kill each other!" Now
that I'm in my late sixties, I have to agree with her. Not that we
would actually kill each other, but close quarters with relatives is
a recipe for tension and conflict. But in the Kingdom Age, we will
be united by our love for God and His ways. Only love and faith
in God can change a sinful heart. Only the fruit of the Spirit can
permit people to live together in harmony and peace.

Verse 3 introduces us to our new Kingdom Age family, and
new home. Earth has been totally renovated. Human attitudes and
relationships are refreshingly different. No family dysfunction. No
tyrants, no abuse, no envy or strife. All self-interest restrained, and
the interests of others is primary. No need for law enforcement or
security systems. Our new home is secure with harmony, mutual
trust, and good will. The 'golden rule' is natural. Honesty and
transparency eliminates suspicion. Father God has anticipated our
every need; The finest furniture, floors, carpets, styles and colors.
Our preferences and options have been pre-arranged, just the
way we want them. Decorations, fireplaces, exquisite statues and
sculptures, murals, winding stairs, just as we desire. Personalized
dinnerware, plates, platters, glasses and cups. Lamps and crystal
chandeliers of the finest quality. Expensive, high-end appliances.
Mealtimes are wonderful times of discussions and sharing of

questions and concerns. Servant angels attend to all mealtime necessities. Beloved pets from our past lives run about, greeting us and respond to our instructions the first time. Family discussions are times of learning, growth and acceptance. A nurturing, loving atmosphere predominates. Family outings and vacations are planned with joyful anticipation. Money is not a factor in heaven! God Himself often manifests to share in the discussions and make wise recommendations for our vacation travels.

In verse 4, we read about peace and harmony in the kingdom age. No pain or sickness EVER, no headaches, colds, flu, joint pain, or, stomach "issues." No more fear, anxiety, or sadness. No more toxic emotions. No more lust, jealously, or rage outbursts. No more personality conflicts, threats, or lawsuits. No more car or plane accidents. No more Ominous X-rays or alarming lab results. The home atmosphere is filled with acceptance and genuine concern for each other. Sensitivity and consideration prevail. All the fruits of the Spirit are in evidence—love, joy, peace, long-suffering, kindness, goodness, faithfulness, gentleness, and self-control.

Verses 6–7 are about the privilege of life, the gift of eternal life, abundant life with vitality and purpose—the family as it was meant to be.

In verse 8, we learn that apparently, some will abuse God's gift of free will and will choose ungodly lifestyles. These "shall have their part in the Lake which burns with fire and brimstone, which is the second death." These people who live during the kingdom age cannot blame Satan as he is locked up in the bottomless pit (Revelation 20:1–3).

Our God is not a neutral, nebulous force; He is active, ever watchful to protect His family. His personality is a balance of justice, mercy, and tough love. Again, this appearance of evil in the midst of paradise confirms what happened in the Garden of Eden. A perfect environment simply will not guarantee a successful outcome. All of us need to be tested and proven. Justifiable consequences await those who trample on God's grace (Hebrews 10:29). Again, the greasy-grace crowd needs to take note. Father God does not need mans approval to define and judge sin.

Verses 9–27 mentions the holy city, the new Jerusalem, which is awesome beyond words. We are allowed to live in God's neighborhood! The actual residence of the Trinity and thousands of angelic servants and other spiritual beings. It is God's headquarter and flagship city. Satan's proud and wicked city, Babylon, has been destroyed. Evil spirits and evil human beings rightfully suffer for their sins. Again, Father God does not need our approval to judge sin.

Wycliffe Bible Commentary (pages 1522–23) reads,

> 'The Holy city has twelve gates ... each gate is guarded by an angel ... the length, breadth, and height of the city is twelve thousand furlongs, or about 1,500 miles. This would seem, upon first reading, to be in the shape of a cube, but I certainly would follow Simcox, and many others, in believing that this is a PYRAMIDAL structure ... the wall is made of Jasper, the city is of gold, the gates of pearl, and the foundations of twelve precious stones ... If we compare the colors of the foundation stones with those of the rainbow, we shall find, I believe, a designed resemblance.'

Salvation Invitation

All Seekers of God, Accept Christ as Your Lord and Savior

1. Admit you are a sinner.
2. Agree with God and turn (repent) from known sin.
3. By faith, believe that Jesus suffered and died to pay for your sins.
4. Prayerfully invite Jesus into your heart as your Lord and Savior.

Prayer

Dear God, I believe that your Son, Jesus, suffered and died on the cross to pay for my sins. Through faith in Christ, I accept Jesus as my Lord and Savior. Thank you for forgiving me and cleansing me from all sin. Help me to live for you and depend on you all the days of my life, amen.

Revelation 22

In verse 1 of Revelation 22, the last chapter of the book, we read, "And he showed me a pure river of water of life, clear as crystal, proceeding from the throne of God and the Lamb." Have you noticed that the Holy Spirit is hardly ever mentioned? Could it be that our new, glorified bodies are permanently tuned and joined to the Holy Spirit? His children have eternal life in them. Recall what Jesus said to the woman at the well.

> 'Whoever drinks of this water will thirst again, but whoever drinks of the water that I shall give him will never thirst. But the water that I shall give him will become in him a fountain of water springing up into everlasting life.' (John 4:13–14)

According to the *Wycliffe Bible Dictionary* (pages 1787–88),

> Water is mentioned in the Bible more often than any other material resource ... water was a symbol of God's salvation (Isaiah 12:3; cf. Jeremiah 2:13, 17:13) ... for Baptism, to indicate the washing away of sin ... to the woman at Sychar, Christ spoke of 'living water' (John 4:10) ... Water is also a symbol of the Holy Spirit (John 7:37–39).

In verse 2 is mention of the tree of life, God, the source of life: "The leaves of the tree were for the healing of the nations." How many medications come from plants? It is no coincidence that trees are very useful to humankind. They are a main source of building materials, energy, canoes, weapons, furniture, fruit, and warmth in the winter and light in the darkness.

Verse 3's "No more curse" This could mean no more sickness or death, no more poisonous plants, snakes, or insects, no more thorns or thistles. Wild animals will no longer be predators; they will be gentle and eat grass, like cattle. But no doubt it will take some time for me to pet any lion, leopard, tiger, or bear. Due to a traumatic event in my childhood, it took years for me to overcome a fear of dogs.

Verse 4 reads, "They shall see His face, and His Name shall be on their foreheads." To me, this could indicates total mutual trust between humanity and God. We are accepted, and we enjoy open access to our God—perfect fellowship.

Verse 7. Apparently, heavenly time is different from our time; verse 7 is from a heavenly perspective. Jesus exhorts us from heaven, "Behold, I am coming quickly! Blessed is he who keeps the words of the prophesy of this book." Dear reader, after the rapture, if you are not saved, you will most likely be going through the horrors of the seven year tribulation period. Other than the ***THREE SUPER SIGNS*** ; 1. The rebirth of Israel as a Nation in 1948 (Matt 24:32), 2. The convergence of multiple signs, happening at the same time (Matt 24:33,34), 3. World Wide Evangelism (Matt 24:14), there is no 'last call' to board the ship of salvation. The Rapture occurs "in a moment, in the twinkling of an eye" (1 Corinthians 15:52). "Behold NOW is the accepted time; behold, NOW is the day of salvation" (2 Corinthians 6:2).

Verse 11. All procrastinators please take note! Listen to the solemn words of Dr. Charles Ryrie, ThD, PhD (the *Ryrie Study Bible*, study notes for Revelation 22:11): "When Christ comes there will be no more opportunity for a man to change his destiny. What he is then, he will be forever."

Verses 18–19 contain a stern warning not to add to, or to take away, any words from Revelation. Some feel this ominous warning applies to the entire Bible. I pray that Father God will bless my efforts to teach and magnify scripture. Prophesy is more than the classic prophetic warnings in the Old Testament. In the New Testament, we read, "But he who prophesies speaks EDIFICATION and EXHORTATION and COMFORT to men" (1 Corinthians 14:3).

CHAPTER 11
Hitler, Obama, and the Coming Apocalypse

Let us look at previous antichrists (small a) and see what they teach us about the final Antichrist. How did they come to power? What societal conditions were favorable for their acceptance? Was trickery, lies, and camouflage used? Were there common antecedents? The Bible calls them "wolves in sheep's clothing" (Matthew 7:15). How gullible is the current generation?

In my opinion, Hitler and lessor antichrists, were eventually revealed to be devious and lawless agents of radical change. Former President Obama was not a monster, like Hitler, Stalin and others. He (Obama) was civilized and law abiding, for the most part. However, he did express traits of a antichrist, at a much lower level. I will provide documentation as this chapter continues. Jesus described them as 'false prophets', and 'wolves in sheep's clothing', "You will know them by their fruits" (Matthew 7:16). I expounded on this dynamic in my first book, *Mr. President, I Respectfully Disagree.*

I believe there is abundant documentation to show that Obama made use of specious and spurious pronouncements. Lying, accusing, and deceiving (LAD), as stated previously, are biblical names and traits of Satan (see footnote 3, chapter 9). Obama was not a dictator or a murderer. Per scripture, murderer is another name for, and personality trait of Satan (John 8:44). I will provide documentation for what I believe are instances of lying, accusing and deceiving (LAD). The following books and articles are my general sources; specific footnotes are forthcoming.

- *You Lie!* by Jack Cashill
- *Trickle Down Tyranny* by Michael Savage
- *The Psychopathic God—Adolf Hitler* by Robert G. L. Waite
- *1,180 Documented Examples of Barack Obama's Lying, Law-breaking, Corruption, Cronyism, Hypocrisy, Waste, Etc.* by Tim Brown of Freedom Outpost
- *The Worst President in History* by Matt Margolis and Mark Noonan
- *Clean House* by Tom Fitton of Judicial Watch
- *The Roots of Obama's Rage* by Dinesh D'Souza
- *Buyer's Remorse* by Bill Press
- *God, Guns, Grits, and Gravy* by Mike Huckabee
- *Mr. President, I Respectfully Disagree* by yours truly.

I could have listed more books. For example, *The Christian Cleansing of America* by Noah W. Hutchings with Carol Rushton. Also, I recently obtained a copy of David Horowitz's latest book, *Dark Agenda: The War to Destroy Christian America*. Horowitz wrote an entire chapter on former President Obama's contribution to the anti-Christian agenda of the political left. My books and the above listed books were meant to sound the alarm for the current generation. Of course, I am not the only one. Hundreds and perhaps thousands of God's servants are also sensing societal dystopia, and the soon return of our Lord and Savior, Jesus Christ. My emphasis is that our current societal dysfunction is due to spiritual reasons. The current polarization, I believe, is being caused by spiritual forces. These political conflicts are evidence of a spiritual war. These social disorders, and conflicts line up nicely with Bible Prophesy. It is not a coincidence.

Like Paul Revere, God's ministers are pointing to the

convergence of signs that are currently shouting that the second coming of Christ is near. I have enumerated many indicators in this book that we are most likely living in the season of His coming. After thousands of years, the Jews have regathered to their ancient homeland. The prophesied apostasy is strengthening every month. Knowledge, travel, and technology have increased dramatically. Worldwide evangelism has only recently become possible thanks to the prophesied increase in knowledge and technology. Natural disasters including fires, floods, droughts, hurricanes, tornadoes and earthquakes are increasing. Epidemic diseases and drug-resistant bacteria are increasing. Wars and rumors of wars, including preparations for the "Ezekiel 38—39" war are in the news frequently. I believe the *Rapture* is about to occur. The final Antichrist is about to make his appearance. You do *NOT* want to be left behind!

Allow me to highlight just one national sin causing the deep displeasure of Father

God;

'January 22—on the anniversary of the tragic *Roe v. Wade* ruling legalizing abortion—New York Governor Andrew Cuomo signed an abortion bill into law in front of cheering members of the state assembly.'

'What were they cheering? A new law declaring that children could be killed indiscriminately in the womb after the 24th week of pregnancy ... and now allowing for many abortions right up until the moment of birth.'

'Governor Cuomo further celebrated opening this door to infanticide by ordering pink lighting at New York City's Freedom Tower built on the site of the 9/11 attacks. As one observer pointed out, the place where 3,000 innocent people lost their lives was used to celebrate the taking of thousands—and even millions—more innocent lives … My friend, this is simply demonic. God spoke clearly to the ancient Israelites about the evil of child sacrifice.'

"I myself will set my face against that man and will cut him off from among his people, because he has given of his children to Molech". (Leviticus 20:3)

The above quote is from a letter issued by Frank Wright, PhD, President and CEO of D. James Kennedy Ministries dated March 2019.

May I point out that Father God refused to pardon the shedding of innocent blood by Judah and King Manasseh (2 Kings 24:1–4). The nation of Israel was punished severely and taken captive to Babylon. Yet, in our modern era, Governor Cuomo and fellow legislators exhibit raucous glee with expanding this very serious sin.

Jesus Himself gave us many signs and signals alerting us to His second coming (Matthew 24). His prophetic words are reinforced and expanded on in many other scriptures. Regarding abortion, Satan has simply repackaged the sin of child sacrifice. Casual abortion used as 'birth control' is flat out wrong, in my opinion. Modern, sophisticated progressives exhibit blatant disregard for God's laws. Today the sins of Sodom and Gomorrah have become accepted, promoted, and legally protected. Political and legal forces gleefully promote protection for these sins. Eradication of biblical values and symbols are vigorously pursued by antichristian forces. Again, '***SATAN IS LAUGHING***'.

While Father God loves sinners, He will not endlessly tolerate persistent (lifestyle) violation of His laws and statutes. God Himself placed hostility between believers and non-believers. (Gen 3:15) We belong to different KINGDOMS. The degree of mass deception is accelerating. Lot 'offended' the people of Sodom and Gomorrah (Genesis 19:1–13). God's judgments follow apostasy just as thunder follows lightning. He is the sovereign of the universe, the Creator and lawgiver. If those who believe as I do are correct, America is on a collision course with Deity. The book of Revelation assures us of eventual victory, and destruction of evil. Again, fulfilled prophesy strongly confirms the divine inspiration of the Holy Scriptures.

It is true that no one knows the day or the hour of the second coming. However, Father God wants His children to know season of this event. Scripture repeatedly encourages us to be alert for the signs of His return. The current convergence of signs and birth pangs indicates we are "near, AT THE VERY DOORS" (Mark 13:29). Many books by godly men are available. My first book covered less than a dozen of the signs and birth pangs. Like all dispensations, the Church Age has a beginning and an end. It will end at the Rapture, the rescue of God's family. I believe it is very close. Ever-increasing apostasy and severe persecution of Jews and Christians are major *'BIRTH-PANGS'.*

Brethren, notice, I do not set dates for the return of Christ. The Church Age, or Age of Grace, has already lasted almost 2,000 years. What could be holding up the second coming? Many Christians speculate that, when the last person accepts Christ during the Church Age, Father God will call us home to safety.

Again, a major indication as to the nearness of the second coming is in Matthew 24:14: "Jesus said, 'And this gospel of the Kingdom shall be preached in ALL THE WORLD for a witness unto ALL nations; and THEN the end will come.''

> 'This was not possible until modern technology gave us the printing press, radio, shortwave radio, TV, satellite TV, and the computer. Only recently can it be said that the gospel is being preached to all nations. Did you see it?! Our generation has the ability to fulfill this sign. Modern technology has

> only recently permitted this sign to be active and
> fulfilled.' (*Mr. President, I Respectfully Disagree*, 89)

What man is not able to do—worldwide evangelism—Father God will complete. After the Rapture, and during the seven year tribulation period, God will use 144,000 Jewish evangelists (Revelation 7) and the angel who preached the gospel (Revelation 14:6–7). This way, mankind will always have a choice. Earth dwellers can never say "You never told me!"

When you combine the signs and birth pangs of worldwide evangelism, the reemergence of Israel as a nation, the explosion of knowledge, technology, and travel, famine, pestilence, earthquakes, massive deception, and apostasy, there is only one conclusion—we are in the last days of the Church Age. Therefore, the Rapture of believers is ___imminent!___

Current conditions are similar to previous major judgment events by God. These sinful conditions had reached the point of no return (no remedy). Those generations that experienced God's wrath exhibited advanced opposition and defiance. Verbal abuse, contempt, and oppression of the poor were widespread. Eventually, outright slaughter of believers provoked God to action. Deep seated contempt continues to grow towards Jews and Christians all over the world today. We are in a ___spiritual___ war that is being manifested as a political and cultural war.

Brethren, none of us are sinless. We all are 'sinners saved by grace'. We need to be cautious before casting aside a rogue such as Donald Trump. His unique personality is the result of his blend of heredity and environment. Obviously, he is not timid or shy. He was born into a family of 'alpha males'. He is not restrained by usual social customs. At least he is consistent. Listen…."He who is without sin among you, let him throw a stone at her first" (John 8:7).

I repeat, evil and apostasy have grown. In my opinion, the trigger point for judgment is near: "My Spirit shall not strive with man forever" (Genesis 6:3). The New Testament agrees: "The remnant will be saved. For He will finish the work and cut it short in righteousness, Because the Lord will make a short work upon the earth" (Romans 9:27–28).

At the **SECOND** stage of the second coming, Christ will return to the Mount of Olives (Acts 1:11; Zechariah 14:4). At the **FIRST** stage of the second coming He returns in the air, at the Rapture 1 Thess 4:16—18. He loves us! We are not the object of His wrath (1 Thessalonians 5:9). Believers rightfully look for the 'blessed hope'— Christ—not for the final Antichrist and seven years of the wrath of God Titus 2:13.

Look what happens after the Rapture. The book of Revelation explains everything. The final Antichrist deceives and eventually leads gullible humanity to attack Christ Himself (Revelation 19:19). As I type these words, the Rapture has yet to occur. There is still time to accept Christ and avoid His wrath. History is once again repeating itself. Those who know Father God and study scripture, know that His return is imminent.

The same was true for the wise men from the east. They knew the signs of the *first* coming of Messiah. Apparently, they studied the Jewish Prophets, especially the book of Daniel. They calculated 'Gabriel's prophesy of the Seventy Weeks' (Daniel 9:24). The traveled many treacherous miles to Jerusalem and then to Bethlehem to find the Messiah. "Where is He who has been born King of the Jews? For we have seen His star in the East and have come to worship Him" (Matthew 2:2). Apparently, God also spoke to them via astronomy (Genesis 1:14, Job 38:33). By the way, wise men still seek Him.

The Old and New Testaments give abundant information to guide us to important biblical times and seasons. Signs of the second coming are shouting, for those who will listen. That is why Christian leaders are sounding the alarm. Pre-tribulation salvation is still available to "whosoever". Do your own thinking and investigation. Again, the Rapture is the first stage of the second coming. It will happen in the twinkling of an eye (1 Corinthians 15:52; 1 Thessalonians 4:16–17). Did you notice the word *trump* in verse 16 of the King James Version? Is it just a coincidence that Trump is the name of our current president?

I suspect that, shortly after the Rapture of the true church, end-time events will occur in rapid succession. No doubt experts, both 'religious' (FRS) and scientific, will try to explain the disappearance—the Rapture—of millions of Christians. One possible scenario, is that Satan will orchestrate 'alien' (Demonic) 'UFO' landings around the world to announce the arrival of a 'New Age' for humankind'. The apostate church, the FRS, will be used by Satan and the final Antichrist to deceive the gullible. Sin-soaked humanity will be conditioned for such a deception. 'Sophisticated' Agnostics and others, who reject Christ, will suddenly accept and entertain demons. Could this be part of the 'snare" spoken of in Luke 21:35–36? Listen, 'There were giants on the earth in those days, and also afterward, when the sons of God came into the daughters of men and they bore children to them. Those were the mighty men who were of old, men of renown. Then the Lord saw that the wickedness of man was great in the earth, and that every intent of the thoughts of his heart was only evil continually.' Genesis 6:4—5. Could it happen again? Hybrids who appear human? Could the Antichrist be a ***HYBRID?***

The Church Age is over. God has removed His faithful Church from the earth. When the final Antichrist signs the seven-year peace treaty and guarantees Israel's safety, the countdown to Christ's second coming will start. Of course, this will be ruthlessly suppressed. The Antichrist and the False Prophet continually promote distrust and disdain for God. Suddenly, a tiny remnant will realize that scripture is being fulfilled. With fear and consternation they ***now realize*** they are in a very precarious position. Now they will have to navigate the horrors of the seven-year tribulation. To accept Christ now will mean certain death, probably by beheading (Revelation 20:4). But if they take the mark of the beast to survive, they will suffer the wrath of God (Revelation 14:9–10). They will have to join the 'outcasts'. They will have to join the pockets of resistance to the Antichrist. It will not be easy. If you know history, after the fall of France in World War II, many Frenchmen joined the resistance to Hitler and the Nazi's. Scripture describes the sufferings of believers during these tribulation days (Matthew 24:9–27).

Fertile conditions were catalysts for the acceptance of Hitler. Conditions were similar, but to a much lesser degree for Barack Obama. Hitler was a definite precursor of the final Antichrist. No one but God knows the identity of the final Antichrist. If one studies Bible Prophesy, he or she will know what to look for. There is nothing wrong with comparing current events with Bible prophesy. Prophesy can be delayed, but never stopped. Only the Holy Spirit can enable us to discern times and seasons.

May we all aspire to be a 'watchmen on the wall' (Isaiah 21:6). God bless those who are wise and discerning. God bless those who warn others of Satan's schemes and strategies. I agree with biblical scholars who say the next event to look for is the 'Rapture'. The events of World War I, World War II and people like Hitler and Stalin were without a doubt, major birth pangs and signs. Just as there are known signs for a volcanic eruption, or birth of a baby, Christ gave us the indicators and road signs to look for. Again, it bears repeating, the three **_SUPER SIGNS_** previously mentioned, indicate we are "near, at the very doors" Matt 24:33.

The world ruler of the future will possess charisma, gravitas, super intelligence and unmatched powers of persuasion. He will make Hitler and others look like 'choir boys'. By 'intrigue' and treachery, he will work his way up the food chain. The world, and surprisingly, Israel, will be enamored with this man (Revelation 13:3–4). Gradually, he will gain control of the world's religious, economic, and military power. This will provide him with the credibility to offer 'peace and prosperity'. His seven-year peace pact will be applauded as 'Brilliant' and incorporate Israel (Daniel 9:27; John 5:43). But like all tyrants and maniacs, he will bite off more than he can chew. He will eventually show his true character and blaspheme all sources of authority, even the God of the Bible. Humankind will be hopelessly deceived and accept him as 'lord of the universe'. No mere man can stop him. But, earth's true Messiah, Christ Jesus, takes a few seconds out of His day and lets loose with overwhelming power. There is no battle.

> Now out of His mouth goes a sharp sword, that with it He should strike the nations. And He Himself will rule them with a rod of iron. He Himself treads the winepress of the fierceness and wrath of Almighty God. (Revelation 19:15)

Again, so much for the greasy-grace, meek, and mild Jesus.

Former President Obama was not trusted by most of the Jewish population. I doubt they would ever trust him. Of course, this lessens the possibility that he is the final Antichrist. Nor did he ever claim to be god. However, his style, charisma, oratory, demagoguery, and his rabid and faithful supporters, caught my attention. I found his speeches and press conferences full of specious and spurious strategies. In my opinion, he almost always had a hidden agenda. Looking back, I believe Father God was teaching me to teach others how to discern false leaders. Prophesy has been my lifelong passion. Lord willing, I will not be here when the crème de la crème of con artists makes his earthly appearance. I do not handle blood or pain very well. I do not like to think about 'death machines' such as the guillotine.

Both Hitler and Obama started small and were given little chance to achieve high office. At first, no one gave Obama a chance against Hillary Clinton. She was powerful politically and financially. However, Obama was young, charismatic, a fresh face, a minority, and well educated. He became the media darling of academia and the liberal news media. By the way, this (gushing approval) is also going to be true of the final Antichrist, who starts out as the small horn of Daniel 7:8.

> "Dorothy Thompson, one of the very few foreign correspondents who was permitted a personal interview with Hitler, was surprised and disappointed by the "startling INSIGNIFICANCE" of this man who has set the world agog ... He is the very prototype of the 'Little Man,' "she wrote in the spring of 1932 ... Like so many others, she underestimated this nondescript politician and failed to recognize the paradox that part of his power lay in his "startling insignificance" (1). Another related quote states "In 1928 his (Hitler's) party had been a minor splinter group with 2.6 percent of the total vote" (2).

> Hitler's party, the National Socialist German Workers Party, is better known as the NAZI Party. In my opinion, both Hitler and Obama sought to weaken individual rights and make citizens more dependent and accountable to government. Both Hitler and Obama were socialists. According to the Free Dictionary.com, socialism is; Any of various theories or systems of social organization in which the means of producing and distributing goods is owned collectively, or by a centralized government that often plans and controls the economy."

Additional quotes from the Free Dictionary.com regarding socialism include these;

> "The worst advertisement for Socialism is its ADHERENTS (George Orwell)."

"To the ordinary working man, the sort you would meet in any pub on Saturday night, Socialism does not mean much more than better wages and shorter hours and nobody bossing you about. (George Orwell, *The Road to Wigan Pier*)"

"Idleness, selfishness, fecklessness, envy and irresponsibility are the vices upon which socialism in any form flourishes and which it in turn encourages. But socialism's devilishly clever tactic is to play up to all these human failings, while making those who practice them feel good about it. (Margaret Thatcher, Nicholas Ridley Memorial Lecture)"

"The problem with socialism is that eventually you run out of other people's money (to spend)." (Margaret Thatcher, https://en.wikiquote.org/wiki/Talk:Margaret_Thatcher)

Per a letter from D. James Kennedy Ministries received by this writer in February 2019, "Four Undeniable Truths about Socialism,"

1. Under socialism, the state makes your choices for you. Controlling all the goods and services in the economy, the socialist state makes all the allocation decisions. Can you go to college? What kind of work can you do? Where can you live? The state decides all these things for you.
2. Socialism is at war with personal faith and family. Socialist governments do not permit other competing authority structures, hence the rights of families and churches are subordinate to the interests and power of government. Religious freedom? Not so much.

3. Socialism destroys innovation. The stated socialist goal of economic redistribution effectively destroys all incentive for innovation. If everyone's outcome is the same, there is no reward for extra effort. Besides, under socialism, access to capital is strictly controlled, so there is no Google, Facebook, Amazon, Apple, YouTube, or Wikipedia. Try to find an emoji for that.

4. Socialism doesn't work. Here is reality. Government has no money to give to one group that it does not first take from another. As British Prime Minister Margaret Thatcher once put it; "The problem with socialism is that sooner or later you run out of other people's money."

Hitler did not hesitate to use terror tactics to reinforce his control. Of course, Obama was a civilized man who used presidential authority and executive departments (FBI, DOJ, EPA, IRS) to augment his elective privileges. Hitler and Obama were both charismatic; they both made wild promises and used demagoguery to persuade the gullible. Multiple journalists and authors described the supporters of Hitler and Obama as having religious and messianic fervor. Regarding Obama, "There was something 'messianic' about the candidate. In our eyes and dreams, Barack Obama ... was, indeed, 'THE ONE'" (3).

Another frequently cited quote of Obama has a messianic flavor.

> That night he (Obama) told a crowd of supporters in St. Paul, Minnesota; "We will be able to look back and tell our children that this was the moment when we began to provide care for the sick, and good jobs to the jobless; this was the moment when the RISE OF THE OCEANS BEGAN TO SLOW AND OUR PLANET BEGAN TO HEAL." (4)

A well-known TV personality, Barbara Walters, said of Obama, "We thought he was going to be THE NEXT MESSIAH." (5)

All prophesy enthusiasts took note when the January 18, 2013 edition of *Newsweek* magazine had on the **FRONT COVER** a picture of Barack Obama with the caption "THE SECOND COMING."

Both Hitler and Obama were described as peculiar. Hitler was described as "warped, banal, and peculiar" (6). One book described Obama as "strange, narcissistic, and divisive" (7). Another book reported, "Pulitzer Prize-winning political cartoonist Pat Oliphant depicted the new president as a cold, distant, aloof, an inscrutable Easter Island statue" (8). The word **COUNTERFEIT** was used by a college professor to describe Obama in the same book (9). Still another book quoted *Newsweek* writer Evan Thomas as describing Obama as "slightly creepy" and "deeply manipulative" (10).

Both Hitler and Obama had issues with their biological fathers. Obama's father reportedly abandoned his family and was an atheist (11). If true, that would make Obama Sr. an infidel per 1 Timothy 5:8. Yet, Obama deeply identified with his absentee father and strongly held his father's dreams and goals, per Dinesh D'Souza (12). The younger Obama internalized his father's anticolonialism and disliked rich capitalists as oppressive and exploitive of Third World countries (13). Recall Obama's lukewarm attitude toward American exceptionalism (14). Recall the missing bust of Winston Churchill. Per Dinesh D'Souza, "In the 1950's Churchill was prime minister during Britain's fight against the Mau Mau uprising in Kenya, the native country of Obama's father" (15). That might help explain Obama's attitude toward capitalism and colonialism. I must agree that abuse and exploitation of others is wrong.

Both Obama and Hitler sought to target perceived enemies and inflame feelings of victimization (16). Specifically, Hitler blamed and accused (LAD) the Jews, the Allied victors of World War I, and the Treaty of Versailles, for Germany's sad condition (17). The terrible inflation of 1923 and the Great Depression of 1930–33 greatly exacerbated suffering in postwar Germany (18).

Regarding Obama, he repeatedly blamed (LAD) former President Bush and republicans for America's economic woes and did so deep into his term as president (19). Obama was a divider and stirred up strife and division by repeatedly playing the race card and the class card—rich vs. poor—(20). "Brethren, note those who cause divisions and offenses, contrary to the doctrine which you learned, and avoid them" (Romans 16:17). At times, Obama was critical of law enforcement, which played well to some segments of America (21). I must agree that there are 'bad actors' in every field and profession. He blatantly favored illegal immigrants over law-abiding, tax-paying citizens (22). Obama repeatedly exhibited hostility and anti-Christian bias while at the same time showing favor to Muslims (23).

Obama and Hitler used socialistic means to restrict individual freedom. Eventually, both enjoyed favorable national news coverage and were warmly approved of by academia (24). Of course, Hitler used Gestapo tactics to intimidate and dominate. Obama in a less pathological manner politicized (Weaponized) executive departments including the IRS, FBI, EPA, and DOJ. Again, both Hitler and Obama were charismatic and promised near utopias if citizens simply trusted in their vision. However, like all socialists, their pie-in-the-sky promises never materialized.

For Germany, the trust in Hitler resulted in the loss of World War II and the total devastation of Germany. For Obama, the results were not as bad—multiple scandals including IRS and Benghazi. More scandals may be forthcoming as President Trump struggles with the 'Deep State'. Also, Obama's preference for Islam, included shielding Muslims, at the expense of Military veterans by calling the Fort Hood shooting "workplace violence."

His administration continued federal funding for anti-Christian causes such as abortion and gay rights. Shovel-ready jobs were found to be not shovel-ready. The Obama era is known for sluggish economic growth, socialized medicine (Obamacare), and non-transparency. As documented previously, the Obama administration made contradicting words and deeds regarding lobbyists. Author Bill Press wrote an entire book titled **BUYER'S REMORSE, How Obama Let Progressives Down.** In my opinion, both Hitler and Obama were superb liars and deceivers (LAD). Sadly, the news media and academia were willing accomplices. I have no doubt that satanic forces advanced during the Obama administration. Social conditions continue to prepare the world for the 'Great World Leader.' Subsequently, the Antichrist will promote his own religion, essentially a satanic trinity. The old establishment along with Judeo-Christian values are in freefall. In my opinion, only faith in God and Holy Spirit discernment can 'break the spell'. Yet people of faith are ridiculed. In some countries, they are slaughtered.

Hitler and Obama excelled at demagoguery and manipulation. Both profited from inexperienced and naïve youth groups (25). Both benefited from those dissatisfied with the establishment and traditional values. Again, regarding Lying, Accusing, Deceiving (LAD), Hitler blamed the Jews and the Allied victors of World War I. Obama blamed (LAD) republicans, oil and coal companies, the wealthy, and the military. Environmentalism became a favorite of the left (26).

Hitler was accepted during a time of extreme national trauma, crisis, and chaos. I believe the final Antichrist will make his move during similar worldwide turmoil. He will be a master manipulator who exploits every opportunity. Scripture indicates he will use 'intrigue' and treachery to ascend to power. People are more vulnerable during times of extreme crisis and trauma. Hitler offered leadership, encouragement and solutions for the country's poverty, suffering, and humiliating loss of World War I. He masterfully managed the sick German economy back to health. He eliminated out-of-control inflation along with extreme hunger and suffering. He greatly revived the military pride of Germany, and brushed aside the humiliating burdens of the Versailles Treaty.

As stated previously, Hitler achieved power in Germany by

intrigue and treachery. Scripture states the final Antichrist will do the same thing, by *intrigue*. Different Bible translations use different words. I know of at least four scriptures (Daniel 8:23, 11:21; Hosea 7:6; Jeremiah 20:10) that use the word *intrigue*. Professor Robert Waite, who wrote *The Psychopathic God—Adolf Hitler*, used that word (intrigue) to describe how Hitler maneuvered into power. (see pages 343—347) I do not know if he knew that word was used in the Bible, to describe the final Antichrist.

Obama on the other hand came to power as a freely elected president. I have said many times that it greatly perturbs me that such a left-leaning socialist was freely elected **TWICE** by American citizens. It says a lot about the moral state of our country. Randall Terry said, "Fool me once, shame on you. Fool me twice, shame on me" (27). Though conservatives made sure America knew of his socialistic leanings, he was re-elected. Though his anti-American mentors, educators, and associates were exposed and his tax-and-spend deficit spending was exhibited, he was re-elected. Even though his anti-Christian actions and pro-Islam actions were there for all to see, no matter. His excessive business regulation and increased taxes resulted in a sluggish economy, but no matter. His lack of enthusiasm for American exceptionalism and his apology tour, no matter. His twenty-year association with controversial pastor and friend, Jeremiah Wright, no matter. His associations with, or knowledge of Louis Farrakhan, Saul Alinsky, Bill Ayres, Frank Marshall Davis, and Van Jones did not prevent millions from voting for him. Any criticism of Obama was usually ignored by the mainstream media, or described as 'malcontents by the lunatic fringe'. At the time, America was under the Obama 'spell'.

Only godly discernment enables clear thinking. Americans need to think for themselves rather than swallow the predigested 'news' of the secular media and secular academia. At least visit conservative Christian sites that can still speak without fear or favor. Listen! If we can pass laws that guarantee 'certified organic' food, we can pass laws that guarantee 'certified objective news'.

We should Insist on 'fact based journalism'. Insist on **BOTH SIDES** of the story. Make journalists liable for slander and defamation of character. Journalism should **not be a 'sacred cow'.** They (Secular News Media) sorely need to be regulated, just like Facebook, Twitter, and the rest of them. Toxic and biased editorials should **not** pass for 'news'. Real 'news' should be sterile and objective. After giving the news, then, give editorials 'PRO & CON'. But, label it as *editorial,* not objective news!

You may recall that Obama recklessly ran up the debt more than all the presidents who preceded him! Also, he tried to grant essential amnesty to millions of illegal immigrants, but was stopped by the Supreme Court (28). Border states, including Arizona were restricted by the Obama Justice Department from strengthening efforts to protect the citizens of Arizona (29). Notice I said illegal immigrants, not undocumented migrants; the progressives love to sugarcoat their agenda. 'Open borders' is like **allowing anybody to walk into your home!** America, why do you fall for such nonsense! Can there be any doubt that the not-so-hidden agenda of the Democrats is to grovel for Hispanic votes? The democrats lust for power is the real motive. We are approximately 21 trillion dollars in debt, yet the Democrats want to open the floodgates from all of Mexico and Central America. Again, they wrap themselves in the robe of humanitarian motives. Common sense and discernment reveal their true motives.

America, shake off the toxic liberal bias in the news and entertainment elites. With Obama came more burdensome taxes, expanding government intrusion, abuse of power, decline of the military, and a decrease in economic strength of the middle class. Some say the tentacles of Obama's shadow government are trying to thwart our new president and impeach him! Instead of working with the Senate and passing legislation for infrastructure, opioid issues, affordable healthcare, immigration, and Homeland Security, they are focused on destroying Donald Trump. What the progressives forget is that all men have flaws, even Bible characters, including King David, Samson, and Paul. But God has, and will, continue to use imperfect men, who repent and move on with Him.

Both Hitler and Obama had issues with their biological fathers. Hitler especially was probably scarred emotionally by his biological father. If Professor Waite was accurate in his research, Hitler's father was a tyrant and sadist. I have heard many horror stories from mental patients over my thirty-plus year career in mental health. The following ranks high in the category of dysfunctional families.

"Alois (Schickelgruber) was Hitler's father. His career in the Austrian bureaucracy had been eminently respectable. After nine years of service, he had achieved the title of senior assistant customs official, and by 1892, he had been promoted to a higher collector, the highest rank open to a man with only an elementary school education. Frau Horl,,who worked for Alois as a cook, testified that he (Hitler's father) was a very strict man with a terrible temper. He often beat the dog until it wet on the floor. He often beat the children, and on occasion beat his wife, Klara. He was accustomed to calling his son Adolf, not by name, but by putting two fingers in his mouth and whistling for him as he did for his dog "(30).

"As is the case with all little boys, Adolf's image of his father was heavily influenced by the picture he had of his father's sexual relations with his mother. For Hitler, this memory was traumatic because as we shall soon see, Adolph at age three had seen—or imagined he had seen—his drunken father rape his beloved young mother" (31). This traumatic childhood event is later examined under the title "Hitler's Primal Scene Trauma" (32). After reading most of Waite's book, I think that the description of sadistic tyrant is a good fit for Hitler and his father.

Some say Obama was narcissistic, but Hitler was much worse. It seems to me that Hitler had traits of at least three personality disorders: paranoid, borderline, and antisocial.

To be fair, we all have shades or traits of different personality types, but most of us do not deviate significantly from social norms. However, Hitler was a ___MONSTER.___

CHAPTER 12
Antichrist and the Apocalypse

Finally, I want to put forth my speculation as to how the final Antichrist might ascend to power. Only the Holy Spirit can enable a person to speak for God; I am trusting God to guide my thoughts as I write this book. Therefore, the entire book, especially the following, is speculation, with no claim of direct inspiration. I believe the final world leader will follow the pattern of Hitler. That is, the Antichrist will make his move during and after severe international traumas. These world wide traumas are going to happen in the exact order as portrayed by The four horsemen metaphor (Revelation 6).

Due to severe wars, economic collapse, famine and disease, mankind will be traumatized and dazed. There will be an urgent need for a 'savior' to return stability and sanity. Remember the prophetic statement by Paul-Henri Spaak, former prime minister of Belgium, first president of the UN General Assembly, and one of the early planners of the European Union.

> "We do not want another committee. We have too many already. What we want is a man of sufficient stature to hold the allegiance of ALL the people and to lift us up out of the economic morass into which we are sinking. Send us such a man, and whether he be God or devil, we will receive him." (1)

Many will jockey for leadership due to severe suffering resulting from war, economic failure, famine and disease. One rather inconspicuous statesman stands out. Smart planning along with fair distribution of resources is the signature strategy of Frank Meyers. Other countries covertly allow unfair advantage by the elite. However, the common classes will no longer tolerate this, and demand reforms. Food riots and looting are common. Frank Meyers is the only politician trusted to oversee reforms. Various alliances are formed. Financial and military groups compete for dominance. Often, the infighting leaves the region worse off than before WW III. The results of Frank Meyers policies continue to shine. There are multiple meetings of Global billionaires and corrupt military leaders. They think they can control Prime Minister Meyers, while retaining his services. Agreements and deals are worked out in Rome, London and Paris. America is a basket case and a non-factor. Many establishment Statemen refuse to cow-tow to the international cabal. However, Frank Meyers has been a minor player in the 'club' for years. The major issue at large is anarchy going on all over the world. Law and order is non-existent in many parts of the world. Israel is no longer restraining its military against surrounding Muslims countries. No one has been able to solve this problem.

After months of difficult bargaining, amazingly, a deal is worked out! It will take billions of dollars in bribes, political deals, combined with guarantees of military commitments. The **_SEVEN-YEAR_** Peace and Security Treaty is finally agreed upon. This treaty is a World Wide Treaty. It essentially carves up Europe into one 'United States of Europe'. It includes the middle east. The Jews can rebuild their Temple within agreed upon limits and restrictions. The Muslims and 'Christians' agree to their land allotments. Frank Meyers is one of the negotiators. Once again praise and honor is heaped upon this man. I believe this world wide treaty covers other nations seeking protection from local 'War Lords' and ruthless Russian and Chinese 'Leaders'. Israel will foolishly trust this man, who may be of Jewish decent. Frank Meyers is voted 'temporary' leader of the new Revived Roman Empire. Only devout Jews and Christians realize that **_Antichrist_** has been revealed. However, due to fears of reprisal, believing Jews and Christians will quietly and cautiously take note of **_"FRANK MEYERS"._** In the middle of the **_SEVEN YEAR TREATY,_** which includes Israel, this man will make a pompous entrance into the Jewish temple and declare himself God (Daniel 9:27; 2 Thessalonians 2:3–4). In shock and disgust, the children of Israel will be forced to "flee to the mountains" (Matthew 24:15–22).

Again, the following is speculation. Who can deny that humankind is currently facing perilous times? (2 Timothy 3:1). Satan knows his time is running out: "Woe to the inhabitants of the earth and the sea! For the devil has come down to you, having great wrath, because he knows that he has a short time" (Revelation 12:12). In spite of this, he continues to vigorously deceive all that he can. There is not one ounce of decency in him. I believe that **_just before_** the sneak attack on America (World War III), Father God will protect His believing remnant via the Rapture (1 Thessalonians 4:16–18, 5:3; Luke 21:34–36). Again, this is the blessed hope of Titus 2:13. Pretribulation adherents are looking for the blessed hope, not seven years of God's judgment.

Most prophetic scholars I am familiar with, note that America is nowhere to be found in prophetic scriptures, at least not directly. Something happens to remove the United States as a major player in Bible prophesy. The following is only one possible scenario.

In my opinion, Vladimir Putin is driven to reconstitute Russia as a superpower. He will exploit any weakness to achieve his agenda. He sees America as a corrupt and declining. Also, America is a severely divided nation. Tired of waiting, Putin conspires to make his move. He recently claimed to have missiles that the 'no one' could shoot down. If true, that would enable a first-strike capability. But, he fears the fleet of nuclear submarines.

Let's say he and his allies (Islamic, German?) plan a surprise attack against America and Europe. The surprise attack will probably include neutron bombs and EMP weapons (Electromagnetic Pulse). These weapons kill thousands and 'fry' electrical circuits. This neutralizes substantial military and communication abilities. Wisely, his plans will include Europe's strategic centers. Possibly, Islamic allies will assist with planting these nuclear bombs in Europe and America. American and European retaliation via nuclear submarines can be mitigated, but not stopped.

In spite of uncertainties, Putin and his gang spend many months planning, refining and including redundancy and back up contingencies. They realize there will be no turning back once the missiles and bombs go off. The target date arrives. Nefarious plans are launched! News and intelligence agencies gradually report in; ___success after success!___ The surprise attacks leave America and Europe paralyzed and quivering like a mortally wounded body. Radioactive gases drift about devastated cities.

After seventy years of the good life, it's back to the horse-and-buggy age. Suddenly, the United States is a Third World country. Without electricity, nothing works. Food spoils, toilets do not flush, and only candles and oil lamps provide light. Smart TV's, computers and phones, are essentially worthless. Government agencies including law enforcement are no longer available. America would not listen! Its people ignored repeated warnings from experts of all types, including, 'doom and gloom' preachers. Grocery stores, pharmacies, gas stations, and department stores are looted. But a curious phenomenon occurs just before the surprise attack on America and Europe. Millions of people **DISAPEAR!** Initially, this event is mixed in with all the other world news headlines. It is soon will discovered that all the missing were devout Christians.

Memories start flooding in. Those left behind start talking; "My mother and grandparents talked about God removing His people from the earth just before the seven-year tribulation period. Remember those books and movies about those who were 'left behind'? Remember that preacher who talked about the end times.

We thought it was just weird religious stuff. We thought it was just doom-and-gloom bible thumpers. But it happened just like they said! If the Rapture was true, what else is true? There may be a scientific reason they disappeared. Lets not go off the deep end with all that religious stuff." However, some people start *discretely* researching 'Bible Prophesy'.

The reality of the sneak attack returns. Structured society begins to unravel. A mass exodus from the jails and prisons means anarchy in the streets. Desperate people and wild dogs roam about. There is no law and order. If you do not own a gun, you are vulnerable to dystopian barbarians. America develops into small groups ruled by local 'warlords'. Farms develop with armed guards. Food is the new gold.

Europe suffered only moderate damage compared to America. NATO survives as the only viable defense against enemies of democratic nations. With America out of the picture, realignment of the power structure begins in earnest. In the face of Russian, Islamic, and Chinese ambitions, Europeans are forced to consolidate and cooperate. The race is on for American military technology. An exodus of scientists begins, but this time, from America, to Europe. Thank God American submarines and European forces launched enough nuclear weapons to degrade Russian and Islamic forces. The Chinese are watching and declaring sovereignty over nearby islands and far eastern countries.

A rush to grab American military assets and technology quickly escalates. The majority of American society lies in ruins. European, Canadian, and former American military leaders scramble to secure and safely transfer these assets to Europe. South American countries are supportive of Europe over the ruthless leaders of Russia and China. All the while, without electricity and technology, America deteriorates into anarchy and fiefdoms. The very old and very young die off first. Those who have farm skills and military experience have the best chance of survival. Printed money, stocks and bonds, luxury homes and cars are essentially worthless. Chopped wood, agriculture, food preservation and farm animals become a high priority. The proper storage of meat and vegetables becomes essential. Europe is quickly recovering and strategically safeguarding its military and infrastructure. They have enough military assets to keep hostile countries at bay. None of this takes Father God by surprise.

Remember Frankie, the boy wonder in chapter 1? He is no longer a child with ODD (Oppositional Defiant Disorder) ; he is now Prime Minister Frank Meyers (a fictitious name). He has transformed his small European country into a political and economic model. He has demonstrated an unusual ability to foresee and resolve social problems. He has a track record for turning around failing companies and is known as an economic wizard. His relatively small military has performed strategic wonders, and his country has subdued and assimilated three surrounding countries. Prime Minister Meyer's country was especially adroit and successful in the EU's efforts to secure former American military hardware and safeguard transfer of American scientists and technology to the EU.

Years earlier, EU citizens took notice when he (Frank Meyers) fought his country's old corrupt establishment and put in place reforms that benefited the middle and lower classes. He abandoned his career as a physician to deal with the greater ills of his country. He projects gravitas and genuine concern for the masses. He is admired for his philanthropic and humanitarian actions. More than that, he has broken up longstanding corrupt families and their stranglehold on social and economic success. He redistributed wealth according to a merit system and was awarded the Nobel Peace Prize. His country has become an oasis of political and economic success. Also, his family has long been a member of the secretive international cabal.

World War III has totally de-stabilized the power structure. America is gone. Both Europe and Russia are scrambling to recover from a limited nuclear exchange. Both want peace, at least temporarily. Regional wars, economic collapse, food riots, and postwar pestilence prevails. Foreign aid and health care for much of the world is simply not available. Survival mode has taken over. Regional warlords develop all over the world. The pursuit of culture and faith gives way to the pursuit of survival. As always, man without God is an animal.

Prime Minister Meyers schemes and plots his way into the upper echelons of European politics. Publicly, he maintains a good reputation. His propaganda machine is effective. Behind closed doors, he uses bribery and blackmail to bring strategic government officials under his control. Those who resist are dealt with legally, politically, or by whatever means necessary. Word gets around that he (Frank Meyers) is not one to trifle with. Loyalty is lavishly rewarded. His political strength begins to snowball. Again, quoting John Acton, "Power tends to corrupt, and absolute power corrupts absolutely."

Flushed with power, Meyer gives charismatic and electrifying speeches. EU citizens are taken by his passion and 'concern for the masses'. Every speech becomes a mutual love fest. When compared to current tyrants in Russian or China, he is considered a savior. Now he is in a position to entice other countries to join his expanding empire. The carrot is his military ability to guarantee peace and security. Also, his economic coalition is second to none. The stick is to be vulnerable to Russian, Islamic or Chinese tyrants, in other words, to be on the outside looking in. Those suffering under regional 'Warlords' also seek his protection.

His 'peace and safety' strategy works and many nations join his alliance. Gradually, his alliance discards the old name 'European Union' in favor of the bold name; "Revived Roman Empire". His public relations department continues to project a sanitized image. The world has no idea of the atrocities carried out to further his agenda. He is touted as the 'man of the hour', a 'man of peace'. Along with the FRS and the False Prophet, ___a trinity of evil___ begins to take shape. A 'cult of personality' and fanatical believers develops into actual 'worship'. In the fall, at night, during a mass celebration event, **SUDDENLY,** gunshots ring out! The beloved leader has been struck down at the height of his career. It was all caught on camera. Hours later, Doctors in bloody lab coats sadly give the news of his death. The leader of the FRS requests to pray over the body. Within hours a news conference is called. The news conference is given the highest priority and scheduled for the next day at 12 noon. ***AMAZINGLY MEYERS STANDS IN FRONT OF THE CAMERAS!!*** Mayhem breaks out in the room. Many shout ***"HE IS GOD!"*** The leader of the World Religious Organization, (FRS) is dressed in full regalia. He (False Prophet) steps forward and announces that 'the powers of heaven have revived Frank Meyers". This world religious leader (False Prophet) also trumpets that an "important' message" will be given by a new ***communication device*** at 9AM the next day. This '***communication device'*** turns out to be a Robot Idol-Image of Frank Meyers. It has microphones, cameras, speakers and 'artificial intelligence' making it appear alive. At precisely 9AM this huge 66 foot Robot Idol-Image POINTS TO FRANK MEYESS and 'speaks';

"BEHOLD YOUR GOD, ALL WHO WILL NOT ACKNOWLEDGE OUR LEADER AS GOD MUST BE PUT TO DEATH. HE HAS BEEN SENT TO EARTH TO SAVE ALL THAT WILL BELIEVE. THERE IS NONE BEFORE HIM, AND NONE WILL COME AFTER HIM. ALL MUST RECEIVE HIS MARK ON YOUR RIGHT HAND OR ON YOUR FOREHEAD. NO ONE IS PERMITTED TO BUY OR SELL WITHOUT THE MARK OF GOD!

Sixty-six days later; Meyer stands in front of the Jewish temple. World leaders along with the False Prophet are bowing with hands cupped in prayer and worship. Hundreds of cameras and microphones jockey for position. As always, his propaganda department sees to it that lights and lasers light up his appearance. Marching soldiers, parades of Tanks and Missiles precede his appearance. The VIP section is ablaze with the colors **RED-YELLOW-BLUE** and with the symbols of the Revived Roman Empire. Cheering crowds fill the streets and parks. Gestapo police are dressed in striking uniforms ready to arrest any protesters. Under-cover Security Police dressed as civilians infiltrate the crowds. 'Der Führer' gazes about with arrogance. His special display vehicle moves amid adoring crowds. Official Empire banners and flags are waved by cheering crowds. Seemingly, no one on earth can stop the **<u>WORSHIP.</u>**

But, **SUDDENLY,** there appears a stirring in the heavens.

Salvation Invitation

All Seekers of God, Accept Christ as Your Lord and Savior

1. Admit you are a sinner.
2. Agree with God and turn (repent) from known sin.
3. By faith, believe that Jesus suffered and died to pay for your sins.
4. Prayerfully invite Jesus into your heart as your Lord and Savior.

Prayer

Dear God, I believe that your Son, Jesus, suffered and died on the cross to pay for my sins. Through faith in Christ, I accept Jesus as my Lord and Savior. Thank you for forgiving me and cleansing me from all sin. Help me to live for you and depend on you all the days of my life, amen.

Printed in the United States
By Bookmasters